Pathways for Learning

Education and Training from 16 to 19

ORGANISATION FOR ECONOMIC CO-OPERATION AND DEVELOPMENT

Pursuant to article 1 of the Convention signed in Paris on 14th December 1960, and which came into force on 30th September 1961, the Organisation for Economic Co-operation and Development (OECD) shall promote policies designed:

- to achieve the highest sustainable economic growth and employment and a rising standard of living in Member countries, while maintaining financial stability, and thus to contribute to the development of the world economy;
- to contribute to sound economic expansion in Member as well as non-member countries in the process of economic development; and
- to contribute to the expansion of world trade on a multilateral, non-discriminatory basis in accordance with international obligations.

The original Member countries of the OECD are Austria, Belgium, Canada, Denmark, France, the Federal Republic of Germany, Greece, Iceland, Ireland, Italy, Luxembourg, the Netherlands, Norway, Portugal, Spain, Sweden, Switzerland, Turkey, the United Kingdom and the United States. The following countries acceded subsequently through accession at the dates indicated hereafter: Japan (28th April 1964), Finland (28th January 1969), Australia (7th June 1971) and New Zealand (29th May 1973).

The Socialist Federal Republic of Yugoslavia takes part in some of the work of the OECD (agreement of 28th October 1961).

Publié en français sous le titre:

LES ADOLESCENTS
A LA CROISÉE DES CHEMINS
Enseignements et formations

© OECD, 1989
Application for permission to reproduce or translate
all or part of this publication should be made to:
Head of Publications Service, OECD
2, rue André-Pascal, 75775 PARIS CEDEX 16, France.

The years immediately following the end of full-time post-compulsory education are among the most complex and critical in any education system. They are complex because they are affected by a wide range of factors: the nature and output of compulsory education, the diverse needs and aspirations of young people, the changing demands of the labour market, the problems of youth unemployment, the influence of higher and continuing education. The post-compulsory stage is a critical one for the individual since it involves important educational, career and even life choices, and for the system because it forms a crucial linkage between education and the economy.

Member countries have very different institutional arrangements at this stage and are, therefore, confronted with problems specifically related to their own distinctive settings (these general problems were analysed in an earlier report: *Education and Training after Basic Schooling*, OECD, 1985). All countries, however, share a strong interest in and support for qualitative changes, considered essential in coping with the common issues and dilemmas they currently confront at this level. Thus, the aim of the present report is to clarify current curriculum issues in post-compulsory (approximately 16 to 19) education focusing primarily on the structure and content of courses and the qualifications to which they lead.

The report has been written by Geoffrey Squires, University of Hull, United Kingdom, in co-operation with Dorota Furth of the OECD Secretariat. It is based primarily on case studies of eleven Member countries listed in the annex and which have been issued separately as OECD Educational Monographs.

The report is published on the responsibility of the Secretary-General of the OECD.

Also available

UNIVERSITIES UNDER SCRUTINY (1987)
(91 87 02 1) ISBN 92-64-12922-7   114 pages   £9.00   US$18.00   F90.00   DM40.00

INFORMATION TECHNOLOGIES AND BASIC LEARNING. Reading, Writing, Science and Mathematics (1987)
(96 87 05 1) ISBN 92-64-13025-X   270 pages   £15.00   US$32.00   F150.00   DM65.00

EDUCATION AND TRAINING AFTER BASIC SCHOOLING (1985)
(91 85 03 1) ISBN 92-64-12742-9   132 pages   £8.00   US$16.00   F80.00   DM35.00

EDUCATION IN MODERN SOCIETY (1985)
(91 85 02 1) ISBN 92-64-12739-9   108 pages   £7.00   US$14.00   F70.00   DM31.00

BECOMING ADULT IN A CHANGING SOCIETY (1985)
(96 85 01 1) ISBN 92-64-12709-7   82 pages   £5.00   US$10.00   F50.00   DM25.00

COMPULSORY SCHOOLING IN A CHANGING WORLD (1983)
(91 83 02 1) ISBN 92-64-12430-6   150 pages   £8.50   US$17.00   F85.00   DM42.00

* * *

OECD EMPLOYMENT OUTLOOK– (September 1988)
(Chapter 2, in particular, presents new cross-country evidence on youth labour market and schooling activity.)
(81 88 05 1) ISBN 92-64-13122-1   226 pages   £19.00   US$36.00   F180.00   DM69.00

Prices charged at the OECD Bookshop.

THE OECD CATALOGUE OF PUBLICATIONS *and supplements will be sent free of charge on request addressed either to OECD Publications Service,
2, rue André-Pascal, 75775 PARIS CEDEX 16, or to the OECD Distributor in your country.*

CONTENTS

SUMMARY AND CONCLUSIONS BY THE OECD SECRETARIAT	7
I. INTRODUCTION	17
II. THE NATURE OF THE POST-COMPULSORY STAGE	19
1. Differentiation and progression	20
2. Access and responsiveness	28
3. Education policy and the education market	29
III. STRUCTURES AND TRENDS	33
1. Contextual trends	33
2. Structures	37
3. Educational and training trends	51
IV. THE TRIPARTITE DIVISION	59
1. The relationship between the three tracks	59
2. General education	68
3. Technical education	78
4. Vocational education	85
V. CONTENT, PROCESS AND STRUCTURE	97
1. The content of courses	97
2. The teaching-learning process	108
3. The structure of courses	112
4. Final remarks	118
NOTES AND REFERENCES	120
Annex: LIST OF COUNTRY STUDIES	122

SUMMARY AND CONCLUSIONS

by the OECD Secretariat

The aims of the report

The purpose of the report is to *clarify* current trends and issues in post-compulsory education; and to do so by focusing on the *curriculum*, i.e. the organisation and content of studies, drawing on the *concrete* experience of a large number of OECD countries. The report grows out of previous OECD studies in this field, in particular *Education and Training after Basic Schooling* (1985), and also draws on other current studies of post-compulsory education which are concerned with the education/economy interface and provision for the disadvantaged.

The term post-compulsory here refers to that stage of education and training that follows immediately after basic full-time compulsory schooling and caters to the needs of young people in the 16-18/19 age group. Typically, it encompasses upper secondary schools, or the second cycle of secondary education, formal youth and further education programmes, apprenticeships and other established out-of-school training programmes, including those on a part-time basis. With a few exceptions (e.g. Canada, United States) post-secondary institutions are not included.

The nature and provision of post-compulsory education need to be clarified because this remains a complex, confusing and poorly conceptualised sector of education. There exists a great body of thinking about the nature and purposes of both compulsory schooling and higher education, but the post-compulsory stage seems to have fallen between these two stools. Indeed, in some countries, it is only in the last decade that any attempt has been made to see it and plan it as a whole. There has been no shortage of initiatives, of action; the problem has been to place these in a coherent policy framework.

The analysis in the report is, however, not a purely abstract or conceptual one; it is derived from, and returns to, what is actually happening in a representative sample of OECD countries. The report is based on studies of post-compulsory education in eleven countries (to be precise, eleven systems, since some studies deal with a jurisdiction or a region rather than the entire country) which were prepared by education authorities or consultants from those countries on the basis of a set of common guidelines, and on information relating to the study received from other countries. The report quotes extensively from the studies, and indeed one of its hidden aims is to lead readers back to them, for they provide a rich account of current developments and issues in the relevant countries. The country studies, issued separately as OECD Educational Monographs, are listed in the Annex.

The report concentrates on the organisation and content of studies, the curriculum. Much of the writing on this sector or stage of education has been concerned with the pattern of institutions. Yet the curriculum lies at the centre of our concerns; it is "the stuff of education".

It is not always easy to disentangle curricular issues from organisational factors on the one hand, and the process of teaching and learning on the other, but the report addresses the two basic questions of the curriculum: what is taught? what ought to be taught? The answers to both questions are far from simple, but that is all the more reason for exploring them.

The report is aimed at a relatively wide audience. This is because there are many policy actors involved in education at this stage, more so perhaps than in any other. The role of central government may itself be shared between several ministries, and there is frequently a regional or local government dimension as well. Employers, higher education institutions, professional bodies, trade unions, parents and students are also involved, and the practitioners in the system often have considerable discretion in the way they interpret and implement policies. The report attempts to provide a common language and framework which can aid debate and negotiation among these various partners, to set national policies in a wider, comparative perspective, and to cite concrete examples which may be useful in forming judgements and planning provision.

All this suggests that the report has an indirect rather than direct bearing on policy, and this is largely true and necessarily so. It is concerned as much with the policy questions as with the policy answers, which are inevitably contingent upon national frameworks, traditions and priorities. Nevertheless, it may be useful in this summary to draw out seven main points which have emerged from the study. These must inevitably be generalised and simplified, and the analysis in the body of the report, and also the country studies, refines and qualifies them. Their relevance and applicability vary not only from country to country, but within countries, from one type of education to another, sometimes from one region to another, and over time. As such they must be treated with due caution.

Changes in general, technical and vocational education

The institutional map of post-compulsory education varies greatly from country to country. In some of the countries in this study, the majority or near-totality of the age group are provided for by a single, comprehensive type of institution, such as an upper secondary school or college; this is the case in Canada (Quebec), Japan, Sweden, Yugoslavia and the United States, although in the case of the last country, the essential choice point comes at the end of secondary, rather than compulsory, education. At the other extreme are countries where the majority of young people enter apprenticeships (which involve both on-the-job training and part-time education) at this stage; this is the situation in Germany and Switzerland. In the remaining countries in the study, France, Italy, the Netherlands and the United Kingdom (for which there are separate studies for England/Wales and Scotland) there is a more mixed or pluralistic pattern, which involves schools, colleges, apprenticeships, training schemes and other special programmes, often for the "risk" groups.

However, the curriculum map varies less from country to country than the institutional one. Previous OECD studies have suggested that at this stage, the curriculum typically subdivides into three main types: "general" education which leads naturally, though not exclusively, to higher education; "technical" education, which equips people for middle-level technician-type jobs; and "vocational" education and training, which prepare for skilled or semi-skilled work. This tripartite typology was taken as the point of departure for this report in an effort to explore to what extent it still holds true and is appropriate to the changing socio-economic developments of modern industrialised societies.

The evidence from the case studies suggests that while these divisions are still apparent in a number of countries, they have been modified in several ways and are likely to be further eroded in the future. The report gives examples of how each of these streams is changing and of the increasing subdivisions within and overlaps between them. *General streams* have in some cases expanded, but in so doing have become more clearly sub-divided, either by subject group (e.g. maths/non-maths, science/arts, for example in Quebec or Sweden) or destination (higher education/employment, as in England/Wales and Switzerland). The apparently homogeneous general stream in Japan in fact contains important sub-types frequently related to ability level. In some countries, such as the United States, a distinction is made between the more prestigious "academic" college preparatory courses or subjects on the one hand, and general courses on the other. It is arguable that in some countries in Europe (e.g. France, Germany and the Netherlands) "general" streams are not in fact general by any reasonable definition, but rather a foundation stage in a long-cycle academic or professional education which reaches its completion only at or after first degree level.

The report highlights the fact that at the post-compulsory level it is the general academic-type streams which are often the most resistant to change. This is not merely due to pressures stemming from higher education requirements but also, and perhaps more fundamentally, to the formal status of the traditional qualifications (e.g. *Baccalauréat, Abitur, Matura*) to which they lead. Since these qualifications often grant legal right to entry into universities, the reforms do not depend so much on the institutions themselves as on government policy concerning the status of these qualifications and the articulation between the two levels.

The changes in *technical streams* seem to be due more to changes in technology than in education. Technology may in fact provide a new centre of gravity for studies at this stage. The specific technologies of the past, concerned with particular elements and processes, are now being subsumed under the more generic systems technologies of information and control: technology is transcending the technical. While distinct technical streams and qualifications still exist in some countries, it is becoming increasingly difficult to distinguish between technical and general education at the top (more theoretical) end and between technical and vocational at the lower (less theoretical) end. The influence of technology does not necessarily result in larger technical streams, though in Italy and Sweden these have grown; rather, it is beginning to permeate the content of all streams or tracks at this stage, and to occupy a major place at the post-secondary level as well.

Significant changes have taken place in previously well-defined *vocational streams*. These are due to a number of factors. In the first place, with rising participation rates at this level, particularly of "new groups", expansion has itself led to growing differentiation within this sector. The attempt to improve, upgrade and increase the attractiveness of vocational courses has entailed at the top end a blurring with the technical streams mentioned above. In some countries broader-based courses have been developed to meet the need for flexibility and substitutability in the labour market. Other countries have stayed largely with a more specific pattern of training which arguably develops transferable skills in terms of work processes (attitudes and approach) if not always of work content. As a result of economic change, the traditional distinct craft-based occupations and their related training have declined. Multi-skilled training for the service sector has grown. Vocational streams have also borne the brunt of youth unemployment and measures to cope with it have affected vocational education more than any other sector at this stage. Indeed, courses labelled vocational are often included at the lower end of the post-compulsory spectrum, but which are essentially remedial, recuperative or with a narrow skill training orientation rather than vocational in the traditional sense of the word. In some countries (e.g. Sweden, United Kingdom) this has led to the emergence of dual or parallel systems of provision.

Thus, a general blurring of the tripartite structure seems to be happening, due to a combination of factors: greater fluidity and uncertainty in the labour market; less rigidly linear access to higher education; the development of continuing education; the problems of youth unemployment; and a declining age group. *It is not that post-compulsory education is becoming less differentiated, but that the basis for differentiation is shifting, the pattern becoming more complex, and the situation more fluid.*

Differentiation, progression and equality

These developments imply that post-compulsory education is likely to remain a highly differentiated sector of education, both vertically in terms of status and level, and horizontally in terms of the scope and specialisation of courses. Its proximity both to the labour market and to higher education, both highly selective, suggests that even comprehensive institutions at this stage are likely to have sharply differentiated curricula. And the fact that systems are catering for an increasing percentage of the age group suggests that diversity of and within provision is likely to become more, not less, important. *A key and perennial question is the extent to which it is possible to develop choice and diversity at this stage whilst keeping to a minimum the well-known negative effects of educational differentiation,* i.e. the development of rigid, socially-biased hierarchical systems and their discriminatory effects in terms of the future educational and career opportunities open to graduates from different streams.

Recent trends in vocational education may serve to illustrate these difficulties. On the one hand, greater emphasis on achievement criteria in determining choices and selection has not drastically changed the social composition of the student body in the different types of courses. In addition, the tendency to steer low achievers and/or low-ability students towards vocational courses has frequently counteracted efforts to raise the status and prestige of vocational credentials. More recent developments also show the difficulties of achieving egalitarian goals. At first sight, for example, the fact that some countries have succeeded in recent years in having more middle-class students in certain vocational streams and a higher proportion of working-class students in general education may be viewed as a positive development. However, different conclusions can be drawn when it is seen that quite often the privileged groups tend to concentrate on those vocational streams which open up better opportunities for employment, whereas many of the less privileged groups enrol in general education as a second choice, because of lack of places in the more rewarding, selective vocational options. Such developments reveal the importance of student strategies – particularly from the middle and upper social strata – in maintaining an advantaged position. The importance and the effects of these strategies are likely to increase in the light of the rapid pace of socio-economic change and the consequent need for, and benefits derived from, making quick, well-informed choices among a vast range of options whose employment value fluctuates. Clearly, this has implications for the *setting up of well-developed information and guidance systems,* and here the potential contribution of new technologies deserves special attention.

The existence of differentiated curricula has at least two other major policy implications. First, although many of the internal differences ultimately reflect socio-economic stratification, thus setting outer limits to the ability of education to pursue egalitarian goals, in one respect education seems to be even more sharply stratified than society. The labour market embodies a much broader concept of human ability than education. The skills and achievements that are involved in successful work go well beyond the cognitive-intellectual ones that are prized particularly in education; they embrace practical, organisational, interpersonal and sometimes artistic ones as well. *This points to the need to re-evaluate the criteria of assessment within education at this stage, to ensure that both access and achievement reflect not only different levels, but types of ability and skill.* Educators are often wary of closer contact with the labour market because they feel this will narrow and constrain the educational process. However, the reverse might also be the case: closer contact with the world of work could broaden and pluralise the criteria of achievement, and ultimately the conception of human potential and its educational development.

Secondly, there is a need to develop a *common currency of qualifications* at this stage which will allow each type of education in a differentiated system to be related to the others, to higher education, and to the labour market. Such a currency, which to some extent exists already in several countries, would allow mobility within diversity, something which is desirable both from the point of view of individual progression, and the optimum use and flexibility of manpower. A common currency of qualifications, expressed in terms of "credits" and "levels", would also allow relevant work experience to be appropriately valued, a point which will become increasingly important in relation to adults.

Transition and foundation

Post-compulsory education has often been described as a stage of transition, between school and higher education, school and work or, in recent years, unemployment. Clearly, it is transitional in many ways: educational, social, legal, economic and personal. However, the concept of transition by itself does not provide a firm basis for planning the curriculum at this stage, although it does point up the need for adequate guidance and counselling, and for flexibility in the access to and sequence of courses in order to accommodate changes of direction in students' educational paths.

The report suggests that the central task of post-compulsory education is to provide a preparation or foundation for a field of work or advanced studies. This foundation is more focused than the general stage of education which precedes it in the compulsory school, but not yet as specific as the specialised education or training which will follow it in higher education or on the job. The duration of these three stages – general, foundation and specific – differs according to the length of the individual's education cycle, which may vary by as much as ten years. Nor are the three stages always distinct: there may, for example, be pre-vocational elements within compulsory schooling, though increasingly these are there for reasons of motivation and orientation, rather than vocational education in the strict sense. And the need not simply to retrain but recycle people's skills in the face of rapid employment changes means that sometimes a whole new foundation has to be laid at a later age.

Nevertheless, the concept of a preparation or foundation stage seems useful in three ways. First, it implies a foundation in knowledge and skills which is sufficiently broad to underwrite work or study in not just one specific job or task, but a range. The nature of that foundation is itself changing. The simple dichotomy between "arts" and "science" is being challenged. The old, specific technologies are giving way to the newer generic technologies of information and systems. The growth of service sector occupations is leading to a greater emphasis on organisational and interpersonal skills. The balance of occupations, and with it curricula, is shifting away from work with things, towards work with information and work with people. There seems to be a greater emphasis on the development of general analytic and problem-solving skills which will be useful in any kind of work or further study.

Secondly, post-compulsory education provides a foundation in terms of attitudes and values. This has long been recognised in traditional forms of vocational and professional education, such as the apprenticeship, which was concerned with inculcating norms, roles, and self-concepts, as well as knowledge and skills. The importance of this dimension of studies has been recognised by educationists who refer to the "hidden curriculum": the norms and messages which are transmitted not only through the content of courses, but the teaching process and learning environment. Likewise, some economists have suggested that there is a "hidden" contract which complements the formal labour contract, and which influences the way people work and the intensity of their labour.

Thirdly, post-compulsory education may provide a foundation in a more personal way, by giving people that sense of competence in a particular field, whether academic or vocational, which is an important aspect of adult identity; the sense of knowing or being able to do something which not everyone knows or can do. Again, the process of identity formation will vary with the overall length of the educational cycle, and for some will be associated with higher education rather than with this sector. At whatever age it occurs, however, the notions of transition and foundation will be closely linked.

What are the implications of this for policy? They bear mainly on the training of teachers, or to be more precise, those who have a teaching role both in and outside education, at this stage. *The training of such people should be informed by awareness of the characteristic features and tasks of the post-compulsory stage: the importance of foundation knowledge and skills; the importance of role modelling and the learning environment; and the need for all who are directly involved with students or trainees to be aware of the problems of information and guidance.*

The structure of courses

The report suggests that post-compulsory education can be regarded as part planned system and part education market. This duality affects not only the content of courses, but their structure, and creates the need to provide both continuity and flexibility. In some countries, courses are organised mainly in "lines of study" which maximise continuity and coherence, in terms not only of the curriculum, but of the student group. In other countries, a more modular pattern prevails, which maximises choice and flexibility, both educational and personal.

It may be that these two patterns will converge more in the future, perhaps towards a "core-option" pattern which attempts to accommodate these conflicting demands. Linear systems may have to loosen up somewhat, by providing more choice especially in their later stages, and modular ones tighten up, by insisting on core requirements. However, the pattern is likely to continue to vary not only from country to country but from one type or stream of education to the other, with the long-cycle general courses maintaining more linear structures which allow cumulative study, and the short-cycle vocational ones tending to be more modular in response to changing and more immediate labour market needs.

The link with higher education

Historically, general streams or tracks at the post-compulsory stage have had an exclusive relationship with higher education, in particular with the universities. This is now being modified in two ways: students from such courses may proceed not to universities or higher education, but to employment; and higher education has diversified its intake, sometimes for demographic reasons, to include varying proportions of older or "non-traditional" students. The case studies show that, in most countries, there exist formal opportunities for students to enter higher education from a technical or vocational base ("second route"), and at a later stage ("second chance"). The existence of such formal access does not guarantee, however, that many students avail of it, or that when they do, do not drop out in disproportionate numbers. In policy terms, it is thus important *to stress the difference between formal access and real accessibility to higher education*, and the extent to which "non-traditional" students are actually equipped to cope with higher studies, and higher institutions prepared to cope with them. Both imply a concern not only with the knowledge base of such students, but their capacity to adapt to a different style of teaching and study, and in some cases to an unfamiliar institutional ethos. Equally important are the admissions procedures, access and orientation courses for "new groups" as well as guidance and teaching both before and after entry to higher education.

The formal steps already taken to pluralise access to higher education are to be welcomed but there still remain some key problems in the articulation between the two levels. From the perspective of the post-compulsory stage, higher education often continues to appear relatively monolithic, and the division between courses which lead on to it, and those which do not, remains a deep one in some countries. It is also clear, particularly in countries where there is a "cultural gap" between the academic world and that of employment, that it is difficult for individual programmes of study to reconcile preparation for higher education and for direct entry into the labour market. The experience with many reforms of technical streams shows that efforts to strengthen the "transfer" orientation to higher education carries the risk of a declining employment value of their credentials: the content of studies is considered less relevant, and qualified school-leavers who do not proceed to higher education, in spite of the opportunities that are offered to them, are not perceived as being the best. *Ultimately, the divide is likely to be bridged by the development of intermediate forms of post-secondary education, not only in the form of short-cycle institutions which many countries have established in recent decades, but also of a more diversified and flexible network of courses and qualifications provided within and outside the formal post-secondary system.*

Diversity and coherence at the post-compulsory stage

If there is one general message that emerges from the report, it is that post-compulsory education has to be both diverse and coherent. The statistics cited in Chapter III of the report demonstrate the continuing expansion of post-compulsory education: one, and in some cases more than one, year of post-compulsory education is now the norm in most of the countries. Such expansion creates a problem. Because post-compulsory education has come to provide for a majority or near-totality of the age group at a relatively late stage in their educational development, and because it is close to both higher education and the labour market, it has to be *diverse*: diverse in terms of aims, content, level, modes of attendance, teaching methods and learning environments. Diversity is provided in different ways in the various countries, not only in terms of curricula and the structure of studies, but also in the pattern of institutional arrangements. The existing patterns vary greatly from country to country but again there may be some convergence in the future.

The increasing element of "theory" in many fields (even crafts which used to be predominantly manipulative) suggests that educational institutions, whose strength this is or should be, will have to continue to play a central role in future provision. Conversely, the costs of equipment and the need to provide young people with a wide range of learning environments, role models, and learning tasks suggests that many "non-educational" resources and settings will also have to be used. Indeed, such resources and settings may be the main means of providing for those young people who have become thoroughly alienated from formal education by this stage.

The need for diversity can create particular strains in systems which attempt to provide for the age group in a single type of institution. On the other hand, post-compulsory education needs to be *coherent* if students, employers and others are to make proper use of the resources and opportunities it offers. This need for coherence is most obvious in countries where the institutional pattern is most diverse. It is also becoming a sensitive political issue in countries where there is a trend towards greater decentralisation of the control and decision-making structures dealing with this level. Growing involvement of local authorities and community representatives in steering curricula towards more immediately-felt local needs could carry the risk of distorting the balance between the response to such needs and to educational and training requirements defined in a broader national perspective. In some countries it is also noticeable that the closer links between training schemes and the surrounding community contribute to a sharper segmentation of youth, between those who pursue a type of training leading to qualifications which are essential for a local labour market and those who seek credentials which are nationally recognised.

The need for coordination and coherence in a diversified network of provision has three implications for policy. *First, at the institutional level, consortia or federations of providers which can ensure a comprehensive service to the age group may have to become more common in the future.* Such groupings may be organised on a local basis, partly in relation to local labour markets, and involve both public and private institutions. However, a national system of credits and qualifications would also be crucial in providing the links in such a system, and a general currency for courses and assessment. *The second is the need, referred to earlier, for a common and commonly-understood currency of qualifications which will allow the various parts of the system to relate to one another and to the outside world. Thirdly, the existence of so much choice and diversity points to the key role of information and guidance, not as something ancillary, but as central to the educational process at this particular stage.*

Culture: The hidden element in the links between education and the economy

A general conclusion drawn at the end of the report is that purely structural comparisons of education systems which focus on the pattern of institutions, courses and qualifications must be interpreted with great caution. Some of the most important effects of education are its less overt influences on values, attitudes and norms: on the *culture*, the way of life. The importance of this aspect of education has been suggested by both educationists and economists. Educationists have pointed out that the formal curriculum is only the visible part of what is taught, and have explored what has come to be called the "hidden curriculum" of courses and institutions: those implicit messages which are embodied and transmitted in what is taught and how it is taught. Such messages can affect attitudes to study, to work, and to different kinds of work, influencing for example the perceived status of different occupations or job roles. Economists, likewise, have pointed out that formal labour contracts are inherently incomplete, and that workers always have a hidden element of "discretion" in how they work. Such discretion is influenced by individual attitudes and group norms. This points *to the importance of cultural variables in economic performance*, although the nature and impact of such variables tend to remain speculative. And of course education has cultural effects that go well beyond the economic, in influencing attitudes to institutions, social relations and current issues.

One of the reasons why post-compulsory education is a complex and interesting field is that it brings together the two broad policy themes that have dominated the last two decades: the concern with education and equality in the 1970s, and with education and the economy in the 1980s. Both of these presuppose a relatively direct relationship between education and society. Both themes remain central to the analysis of this sector of education, but it may be that some of the most important effects of post-compulsory education are indirect rather than direct, affecting the cultural and normative variables which in turn affect both social relations and economic performance. This aspect of post-compulsory education may merit closer attention in the 1990s.

I

INTRODUCTION

During the last ten years, both Member countries and the OECD have produced a large number of reports dealing with those years of education which immediately follow the end of compulsory schooling, and which in most countries involve young people between the ages of 15/16 and 18/19. The number of such reports, and their content, bear eloquent witness to the contemporary importance of what is typically referred to as the "post-compulsory sector".

In many cases, the concern with this stage of education has been prompted by a rapid rise in youth unemployment, a rise due to varying combinations of demographic and economic factors. In some countries, youth unemployment is now declining or seems likely to decline; in others, it remains a serious economic and social problem. But the salience of post-compulsory education is not simply a function of the level of youth unemployment: there are permanent reasons for its importance. It enrols increasing proportions of the age group in most countries, an increase which brings with it not only problems of expansion but also of diversification. It lies at the intersection between compulsory schooling, the labour market and higher education. It typically involves a range of governmental and non-governmental agencies. It represents a crucial stage in young people's lives.

This report grows out of previous OECD reports on this field, and in particular *Education and Training after Basic Schooling* (1985). It builds on and develops many of the themes and issues contained in that report, but it differs from it in two ways. First, it concentrates on the organisation and content of studies, on what is taught, and what ought to be taught. Such questions cannot of course be taken in isolation from other aspects of post-compulsory education, such as the institutional pattern, the arrangements for funding both institutions and individuals, the methods and style of teaching, the provision of guidance, and perhaps most important, the structure of qualifications. But in this report, such factors have, as far as possible, been treated as "contextual".

Secondly, this report differs from its predecessor in being based primarily on case studies of eleven Member countries, prepared either by officials within the relevant ministry, or by experts who could provide an informed view of current trends and issues, often in consultation with the ministry, and on relevant information received from other countries. In fact, it would be more accurate to speak of eleven systems rather than eleven countries: the Canadian study is largely confined to Quebec, where post-compulsory education is structured rather differently from the rest of Canada; there are two United Kingdom studies, dealing with the dissimilar systems in England/Wales and Scotland; and the Yugoslav study refers particularly to Croatia. But in all cases, the intention of the studies was not so much to present a statement of current policies, as to analyse problems and changes in the field, and to relate the general questions identified in previous reports to concrete developments.

The case studies are being made available separately from this report; details of them are given at the end. The purpose of this report is therefore not to summarise them or repeat what they say, but to attempt to draw them together in a broader synthesis. The report divides into four main parts. Chapter II, "The Nature of the Post-Compulsory Stage" attempts to clarify and conceptualise what is often an ill-defined, complex and confusing area of provision. Chapter III describes current structures and trends in this sector, drawing on data provided both by the Secretariat and the authors of the case studies. Chapter IV reports and analyses the developments in general, technical and vocational education described in the case studies, quoting extensively from the studies themselves. While every attempt has been made to check the use and interpretation of these extracts with the authors, there is always a danger in taking comments out of context, and readers are referred to the complete texts of the case studies for the full account. Chapter V explores in more detail the content, process and structure of courses at this stage, and ends with some more general remarks.

All comparative studies of education face certain well-known problems, but this study faced two additional ones. It is well recognised that education systems differ markedly from country to country, as a consequence of differences in historical development, cultural norms and policy emphases. It is perhaps less widely recognised that there are major differences in training systems as well. Some countries have an important tradition of apprenticeship; others do not. In some countries, employers assume the main responsibility for training; in others it is the State, regionally or nationally, which fulfills that role. Since the post-compulsory stage typically involves both "education" and "training" such cross-national differences further complicate the already complex educational differences. Secondly, it was said above that this stage of education has been the subject of many reports in the last decade. Such reports have frequently led to major initiatives, many of which are still at an early stage. In such cases, it is often difficult to describe, let alone judge, what is going on, and the verdict must await time and evaluation. However, the value of studies such as these perhaps lies less in attempting to arrive at general judgements than in describing a repertoire of possibilities (and problems) which policy-makers and practitioners in Member countries can take into account in making their own decisions; in giving a sense of the field which can help throw their own case into relief.

II

THE NATURE OF THE POST-COMPULSORY STAGE

The first problem that confronts any study of this stage of education is that of nomenclature and definition. There are two main ways of defining it: in terms of educational status, and in terms of age, but neither is wholly satisfactory. The distinction between compulsory and post-compulsory is complicated by the fact that the age range of compulsory schooling varies from country to country [16 in all the case-study countries except Italy (14), Japan, Switzerland and Yugoslavia (15), with some inter-state variations in the United States]. Part-time compulsory education follows full-time compulsory schooling for two years in the Netherlands, and two or three years in Germany. And even when education or training do become officially voluntary, there may be such pressures on young people to enrol, from the State, from employers and from their families and peers that it becomes effectively compulsory to continue for at least one year beyond the legal minimum.

Definitions in terms of age encounter similar difficulties. While in some countries there is an identifiable two- or three-year period which can be labelled post-compulsory, in other countries that stage is much shorter or does not exist at all. In Scotland, the stage between the end of compulsory schooling (at 16) and admission to higher education (at 17) may last less than a year for a minority of students. In the United States, many young people pass directly from high school to higher education, and the term post-compulsory is not widely used. In countries where the great majority of the age group continue to be enrolled in school beyond the legal minimum age (as in Japan, the United States and Sweden) the term "upper-secondary" is more appropriate, but in other countries where this is not the case, it suggests a level and locus of study which is simply inaccurate for large numbers of young people. And the term "tertiary", which in some countries can refer to this stage (e.g. in England and Wales) in others (e.g. Ireland) can include higher education.

These problems of definition and delimitation suggest that it may be more useful to think of post-compulsory education not as a definable, institutional sector of education but as a stage in a process which begins earlier and may end, for some students, much later, after the completion of higher education. This process has three related aspects, which together comprise a shift in the relationship between the education system and the society of which it is a part. They are, first, an increasing *differentiation* of provision in terms of scope, level and status; secondly, a decrease in the *distance* between education and society, both in terms of institutions and curricula; and thirdly, a shift from a system that is largely plannable and planned to one which takes on some of the characteristics of an *education market*. These three themes will be explored in turn.

1. Differentiation and progression

Education at the primary or basic stage is in all countries relatively undifferentiated in terms of institutions and curricula. There may of course be private as well as State schools, or schools which attempt to impart a particular cultural, religious or social ethos at an early age; and in some systems the quality or reputation of one's primary school may be an important determinant of one's subsequent progress. But most primary or basic schools in a country cover the same range of subjects – whether they are labelled as such or not – and few stream pupils systematically at this stage, although informal rankings may well exist. As pupils move on towards and into the lower secondary stage, curricular differentiation, in terms of type of subject and level of ability begins to emerge, and this is accompanied, in some countries though not others, by institutional differentiation into different types of school. And as pupils approach the stage where they begin to prepare for public or State examinations, such differentiation tends to become sharper. By the time the post-compulsory or upper secondary state is reached, such differentiation becomes recognisably linked to the division of labour in the society, in terms of the type and level of work, and related social stratification.

The basis, pattern and timing of such differentiation varies greatly from country to country, including the eleven Member countries involved in the case studies, and the whole issue of how and when to differentiate, both "vertically" in terms of ability/level, and "horizontally" in terms of lines of study, and the implications for student choice, has been a major preoccupation – perhaps the major preoccupation – of secondary education policy in the last quarter century. Such issues have both an institutional and a curricular dimension. Systems which differentiate relatively early (e.g. Germany, the Netherlands and Switzerland) are characterised by institutional plurality or curricular diversity; those which differentiate late (e.g. Sweden, the United States) tend to have comprehensive institutions or common curricula. Even the latter, however, may be differentiated in terms of a "pecking order" of notionally similar institutions or courses, as in, for example, Japan.

It is not the purpose of this report to reopen the "differentiation debate" within compulsory education, but rather to see how it affects post-compulsory education, in terms of differences in the content/type or level/stream of studies. Figure 1 suggests that there are three dimensions which need to be considered in any analysis of this field. They are the *educational stage* of studies (general, foundation, specific); the *economic sector* towards which they eventually lead; and the *cognitive level* of studies/work. Each of these dimensions will be analysed briefly.

Figure 1 identifies three broad curricular stages in an individual's overall educational cycle. The general stage, which begins with primary education and continues through to the lower secondary stage at least, provides a broad, general educational base through a range of subjects which typically represent the main types of knowledge and skills which are believed to be important for further academic development, social development or personal growth. Models of general education vary from country to country, but they characteristically lay some kind of claim to essence or balance[1]. The preparation or foundation stage is relatively narrower, though still broad compared to the specific stage that follows it. Students at the foundation stage are given the preparation which will enable them to pursue certain types of study (e.g. arts, sciences, technology) or certain types of occupation (e.g. commerce, metalwork, health care) in subsequent studies or employment. The foundation stage is not limited to courses which are labelled as such (which may be rare, or associated with lower-ability students) but covers all courses which perform this broad, though no longer general function. Thus upper secondary school courses which give entry to certain faculties in higher education perform a foundation function just as surely as those which are labelled

Figure 1. **A MODEL OF POST-COMPULSORY EDUCATION**

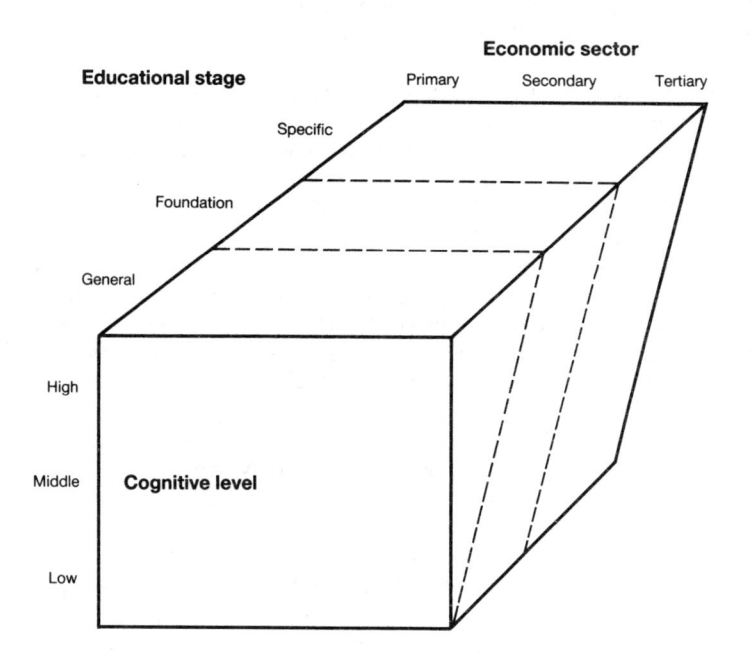

[Figure: A three-dimensional cube model with axes labelled "Educational stage" (Specific, Foundation, General), "Economic sector" (Primary, Secondary, Tertiary), and "Cognitive level" (High, Middle, Low).]

"pre-vocational", and the first year of an apprenticeship may in fact provide a broad foundation for a range of occupations without being officially designated a "foundation year". By contrast, at the specific stage, the course is relatively specialised, either in terms of a field of study (as in higher education) or a particular kind of job. Whereas the previous stages are concerned with preparation and development, specific courses aim at ready competence and expertise in the chosen field or occupation. Beyond that, there may be a fourth "open" stage of continuing education of a wide variety of kinds.

In reality, the pattern for any one individual in any one country is likely to be more complex than this. The stages may blur or overlap, or the sequence be less linear. However, the model seems to clarify several points. First, the duration of each stage depends partly on the overall length of studies. Those who pursue "high-level" studies, leading to high-level occupations tend to continue with their general studies longer than students heading for middle-level or lower-level occupations, and this staggers the subsequent stages. Whereas an apprentice may complete his specific stage and attain competence by the age of 19, specific competence is not reached until the end of post-graduate training in many higher-level occupations (e.g. at the age of 23/24). This helps to explain why in some European countries, the pre-academic post-compulsory stream has historically been called "general"; a fact which makes it difficult to conceptualise and develop models of secondary education which are truly general for the entire age group. Secondly, in some traditional forms of apprenticeship and training, students move directly from the general to the specific, without going through an overt foundation stage, although the schooling element in "dual" systems arguably provides this. This pattern reflects a high degree of stability and definition in the relevant labour market. It should be noted, however, that apprenticeships in Germany, for example, are increasingly sub-divided into four stages of increasing specificity, the first two of which constitute a foundation for work in the relevant occupation, though probably not for a whole lifetime.

More important perhaps than these historical points is the impact of current economic and employment trends on the relationship between the various stages. If employment patterns are both fluid, leading to a breakdown in traditional definitions and demarcations, and uncertain in terms of future developments and needs, the effect may be progressively to transform the "specific" stage into a "continuing" stage. Polyvalence in the job market might be best guaranteed by a combination of a solid, general education, a foundation which lays the basis for trainability in a certain group of occupations, and a greater emphasis on both formal and non-formal continuing education. If such arguments are turned into policies, they tend to conflict with the relatively specialised patterns of both vocational training and professional education at the post-secondary level which have historically existed in some countries. In addition to these natural or at least historical obstacles, such arguments confront two criticisms. First, it is said, the specific stage provides not only an opportunity to acquire knowledge and skills, but occupational socialisation and identity. Secondly, it is argued that the "fluidity" argument rests on an analysis of employment trends which is itself undifferentiated and simplistic. Both these arguments lead on naturally to an analysis of the second dimension of the model, i.e. the economic sectors which represent the first or subsequent destinations of those who have been educated and trained.

The labour market has historically been divided into three broad employment sectors: primary, covering primary production such as agriculture and fisheries; secondary, covering all forms of craft and manufacturing; and tertiary, covering services of various kinds. It is therefore useful initially to distinguish between these three sectors in any analysis of post-compulsory education and its relation to employment. Two general points can be made. First, the balance of employment in the three sectors has changed over time and is still changing. Historically, the high proportions employed in the primary sector (mainly agriculture) have now dwindled to less than 10 per cent in most OECD countries, and less than 5 per cent in the most industrialised ones[2]. The primary sector is now therefore relatively marginal in employment terms.

More significant perhaps for current policies is the current shift from the secondary (manufacturing) to the tertiary (service) sector which is taking place with varying rapidity in the various Member countries. This implies some reorientation or redirection of education and training away from traditional manufacturing industries towards the newer service occupations. This point takes on added significance when related to a second, historical one. The systems of education and training that grew up in the nineteenth and first half of the twentieth centuries related very unevenly to the three sectors. There was some formalised preparation for high-level work in all three sectors, but systematic training for middle and low-level jobs typically existed only for the secondary sector, first in its proto-industrial (i.e. craft) form and subsequently in terms of industrial apprenticeship and training. Despite the fact that agriculture used to be a large employer, it has weak traditions of formal training in most countries, and the skills needed in the various service occupations were, on the whole, acquired on the job. In effect, the historical pattern of education and training formed a capital "T" in relation to the employment market as shown in Figure 1, running across the "top" of all sectors, but with substantial middle-level and lower-level provision only in the secondary (manufacturing) sector.

The importance of this asymmetry is not purely quantitative; it means that the patterns or paradigms of training which have until recently dominated the post-compulsory sector are those which developed in relation to manufacturing industry rather than agriculture or services, and what is more, manufacturing industry at a particular stage of economic and technological development. A comparison may make the point clearer. What if the dominant pattern of formal training in each country had been based on agriculture? Although there are various degrees of specialisation of production within agriculture, in the past it was often a mixed, and therefore multi-skilled activity. Those skills had to be applicable and transferable to a range of conditions and situations. Moreover, farming could require both individual initiative and teamwork. It involved some knowledge of accounting and markets as well as production. In short, a training paradigm based on agriculture might not be very different from the multi-skilled model which is now being advocated as necessary for many service occupations.

However, the usefulness of these broad sector classifications is increasingly being questioned. The classification of occupations is itself a matter of debate. Why distinguish between agriculture and industry when the former has become more like an "agro-industry"? Should mining, which is arguably a form of primary production, be classed with manufacturing? Should construction be classed separately from either? Should industry-based services be grouped with manufacturing, rather than with process or administrative services? It may be useful at this point to list the International Standard Industrial Classification (ISIC) used by the OECD in collecting its labour force statistics.

1. Agriculture, hunting, forestry and fishing.
2. Mining and quarrying.
3. Manufacturing.
4. Electricity, gas and water.
5. Construction.
6. Wholesale and retail trade, restaurants and hotels.
7. Transport, storage and communication.
8. Financing, insurance, real estate and business services.
9. Community, social and personal services.
0. Activities not adequately defined.

It becomes clear from such a list that broad economic sectors may group together activities which, from an education or training point of view, do not necessarily have much in common, a point that is particularly true of the service sector. One cannot assume, for example, that all service jobs involve direct contact with customers or clients; some are as remote from interpersonal contact of that kind as any manufacturing job, and the introduction of new technology can attenuate the contact in others (e.g. automated banking). Some kinds of knowledge and skills (for example communications, clerical, data-processing and managerial) cut across sectors. And changes in the pattern and process of work within occupational groups (e.g. in manufacturing) may be as important to the educator or trainer as changes across such groupings.

The broad shift from the secondary to the tertiary sector does have some consequences for post-compulsory education and training: at a minimum, it implies a rethink of traditional patterns and paradigms of training based on the craft/manufacturing model. But beyond that, what is needed is a more detailed analysis of the nature and structure of tasks within each occupation, and within that from job to job. One tool which has been used in the past for such an analysis is the rating of all jobs in the *U.S. Dictionary of Occupational Titles* in terms of work with information/data, work with people and work with things, in terms of the level of sophistication of each[3]. (Thus jobs which involved primarily manual crafts would rank high on that dimension and lower on the other two, whereas sales work would rate highly on work with people and lower on work with information or things.) Although open to methodological criticisms, such an approach provides a simple tool for assessing shifts in emphasis in occupations and jobs over a period of time.

For example, it is widely argued that many jobs involve more work with information than they used to. The manual craftsman is faced with a wider range of types of materials, and processes for using or transforming them than in the past. There is increasing use of computer numerical control in production processes. Stock control in retail and wholesale firms is increasingly automated. Other occupations appear to have become more "theoretical" or "scientific" and require a better grasp of theory and abstraction than when they relied more on practical know-how: this is the case in agriculture just as much as in some service occupations such as health care. To the extent that service jobs do involve direct contact with people, there is a greater emphasis on interpersonal and social skills; less authoritarian work structures in many occupations make human relationships more important than they were in the past. Conversely, however, work with things (objects, machines) seems to be less important both in terms of the overall shift from manufacturing to services, and also the changes within manufacturing processes, where individually-acquired craft skills (for example in maintenance work) are being supplanted by technologically-based production systems involving flexible work teams. Thus the traditional craft demarcations, strongest in occupations such as ship-building and other heavy industry, seem to be giving way to the need for a more flexible, multi-skilled workforce. Production, innovation and learning all become intertwined[4].

It is important to qualify such generalisations. Some traditional occupations, for example in construction, still seem to require a more traditional pattern of skill acquisition, in which a core skill (e.g. joinery, plastering or electrical installation) remains the essential element. Such a skill may sometimes be subdivided (for example into first-fix and second-fix joiners) and it may be useful for each worker to acquire certain adjunct skills (mainly in order to avoid delays). However, since such core skills are largely manipulative, they require, unlike more cognitive skills, a good deal of practice to be "confirmed", and greater range here would imply less depth. In some high-level jobs, for example in the health professions or financial services, there appear to be trends towards greater specialisation, not less. And the long-term spread of certification means that occupations which were previously open to all comers (for example real estate or travel agency work) are now increasingly regulated and specialised.

The picture is further complicated by the fact that the relationship between initial education/training and employment is sometimes indirect rather than direct. There is hard evidence in some countries, and anecdotal evidence in all, that many people end up doing jobs for which they were not directly or intentionally trained: jobs which are either above, below or different from those envisaged by their initial education/training. Such substitutability, to use the economist's term, is only possible if the labour market is flexible enough to allow it (i.e. absence of employment demarcations and restrictions) but also only if, in some indirect way, the person can transfer what he or she learned for one purpose to a different situation. Subsequent on-the-job learning increases this substitutability. Thus, although there may be apparent mismatches between what the education/training system produces and what the initial labour market needs, the system may continue to function partly on an indirect basis, with young people applying the generic skills (and attitudes) they have consciously or unconsciously acquired to the specific demands of the job. Indeed, advocates of a specific pattern of training at the post-compulsory stage argue that such generic skills are, paradoxically, best acquired through a thorough training in one well-defined field of content, rather than on a broader, intentionally polyvalent foundation course.

What has been said so far presupposes that the sole or prime purpose of post-compulsory education is to prepare young people for the labour market. However, it is one thing to show that people who have had a certain kind of education or training end up in certain jobs (and mobility studies suggest that even this depends on a range of educational, social and employment factors and is not wholly predictable); it is another to say that those destinations constitute the aim or function of education. Policy statements on post-compulsory education typically refer to aims other than economic or employment ones, in terms of education for citizenship, personal development, leisure and so forth. Such aims are widely accepted in formal terms; what really matters is the policy priority accorded to each. In the context of this report, a more pertinent question is perhaps: is education just another service occupation? From the perspective of labour market economics, education clearly belongs to the service sector, although it is in the peculiar position of servicing not only other occupations but itself.

For many educators, however, education is not just another service; it is something which is valued for itself as well as being useful. While such arguments tend to be couched in abstract and perhaps idealistic terms, it is worth pointing out that all "extrinsic" arguments for education logically end up in "intrinsic" concepts as to what is good or worthwhile. In terms of educational policy, the effects of such arguments on the post-compulsory sector are probably to prolong the general stage (in the name of a broad education) somewhat longer than would be justified by strict labour market considerations, and to give a special status to those streams which remain general for longest, i.e. the pre-higher education streams. That status may help to explain the fact, which emerges from the case studies, that such high-level streams appear to have changed less in most countries than technical or vocational streams which are more directly exposed to external influences.

The reference above to level leads on to the third dimension of Figure 1. The term "level" is a familiar one in both education and employment; however, like stage and sector, "level" is a problematic term, to be treated with caution. Although the concept of cognitive or theoretical level is embodied in the structure of education systems, in the admissions requirements of courses and institutions, in the hierarchies of qualifications, and even in terms such as "higher" education, it cannot be assumed that all educational development occurs along a single dimension of ability or achievement. The craft apprentice may be more skilled in some respects than the technician in his field, who in turn may be better at applied problem-solving than the theoretician. The systemic hierarchy of education, which reaches its cognitive or theoretical apex in higher education, in fact coexists with a plurality of abilities which casts doubt on the use of simplistic words such as "high-level" and "low-level" and incidentally on the predictive validity of some entrance requirements for courses[5]. In employment, where the word "level" is also widely used or implied (e.g. middle or top management) the values and measures involved are equally complex, although income provides one overt if crude indicator. Level is apt to be associated not only with knowledge and skill, but with responsibility and autonomy, and with the individual's position and role in the job hierarchy. Furthermore, the relationship between the level of educational achievement and the initial level of employment is a complex one, reflecting factors, such as the general demand for labour in that field, which go well beyond the individual case.

The main policy issue in relation to cognitive or theoretical level is to what extent changes in the vertical structures and relationships of occupations imply corresponding changes in post-compulsory education, modifying either the demarcations between, or emphasis on, the existing types or levels of education. One hypothesis suggests that the demarcations remain, but the emphasis moves away from the lower-level towards middle- and higher-level manpower. This is based on the argument that a general economic displacement is taking place in the world economy, with the industrialised OECD countries being driven up-market by the newly-industrialised countries (NICs) in order to retain market share. This implies a rising threshold of competence in the labour force generally, and a relative or absolute decline in unskilled or semi-skilled jobs. It is also argued that the organisation of work, not to mention social life generally, has become more sophisticated in various ways, and that this also requires a more educated and *cognitively* sophisticated workforce. For example, the flow of information is more rapid than it was in pre-electronic days, the financial aspects of work more intricate, and the legislation affecting employment more complex. Any shift towards self-employment also increases the *cognitive* demands made on workers, to manage their own inputs, processes and marketing, and to deal with the bureaucratic aspects of their work, such as tax and health and safety regulations.

A variant of the "upgrading" hypothesis points to the polarising effects of new technology in certain occupations. Technology upgrades the job where it involves a shift from discrete operations (such as maintaining a particular kind of machine) to systems (such as overseeing a complete input-output process). On the other hand, technology degrades the job where it simplifies an operation which previously required some technical or manipulative skill. Thus it is simpler to replace than to repair a faulty component, or to follow a prescribed decision-making or data-processing routine than to make decisions based on judgement or experience. Since the term "technician" derives from the older technologies, such as mechanical and electrical engineering, it may be a less natural or appropriate category in the newer ones.

The other main scenario involves not so much a redistribution of emphasis among levels of work as a blurring of the vertical demarcations. The traditional distinctions between levels reflect both work hierarchies in specific occupations and more general social stratification. As noted above, the vertical structure of work may be affected by the introduction of new technologies, and new forms of organisation. The conventional, hierarchical categories (such as foreman, supervisor, middle manager, etc.) are so familiar that it is sometimes difficult to see that they reflect a particular kind of industrial or bureaucratic organisation which has been the norm since the middle of the last century. (This is not to say that industrial and bureaucratic forms are similar, but simply that they appear to have originated around the same time.) Just as such forms displaced pre-industrial and pre-bureaucratic forms, so it is possible that new technologies and structures of work will bring with them changes in vertical categories. One currently minor but potentially important example of this is the development of "networkers" who enter into a sub-contractual relationship with the parent company rather than being full-time employees: a kind of half-way house between employment and self-employment. The statistical growth of the service sector (see Chapter III) sometimes disguises the fact that the change is not in what is produced or supplied, but in the contractual relationship. Indeed contracting, in a variety of forms, may be making inroads into conventional bureaucratic structures, ultimately affecting the vertical structures of employment. The broader social stratification is likely to change more slowly, but ultimately reflects the social relations embedded in employment structures.

One further point should be made about the notion of cognitive/theoretical level. It was suggested earlier that the issue of differentiation – both vertically in terms of ability streams and horizontally in terms of programmes of study – has been perhaps the key policy question in secondary education for several decades in Member countries. As the diagrams of education systems in Chapter III show, the issue has been resolved differently in different countries, although such diagrams show only the institutional, not the curricular, pattern. Whatever the pattern, however, the arguments in favour of delayed selection, equality of opportunity, meritocracy and mobility have had an impact on policies in all countries. At the post-compulsory stage, this tends to translate, at a minimum, into an emphasis on opportunities for progression from programmes regarded as having lower status to those with higher status, though the perception of status is of course complex, and varies from country to country. As the case studies show, however, even countries which do not have comprehensive institutions at this stage make deliberate efforts to facilitate, at least formally, such upward educational mobility, through "bridging courses", "second routes", and "non-traditional access". Thus while in many countries the distinctions between different streams of study remain as clear-cut as before, there are, at least on paper, more opportunities to progress, and fewer blind alleys. How successful such initiatives are in practice in increasing progression is a question on which the case studies will throw some light.

The three dimensions of Figure 1 – educational stages, economic sectors, and cognitive levels – thus seem to provide a useful framework for analysing current patterns and policies at the post-compulsory stage. The distinctions within each dimension are not of course clear-cut: one stage can blend into another, there are problems in distinguishing between sectors, and the notion of level is a complex one, both in education and employment. It is important to stress that the model is analytic, rather than normative: it provides an initial tool for analysis, not a prescription for policy. It provides a common framework for describing differences in provision and policy from country to country – differences which may reflect deep-seated historical, cultural and economic factors. One further point should be made, however, on the general subject of differentiation, and this has to do with unemployment.

Figure 1 implies that all or most young people emerging from the education/training system at the post-compulsory stage do in fact find employment in some sector at some level. In the case of high-level courses, this may not happen until after the completion of the "specific" stage in higher or post-graduate education; thus high-level streams in post-compulsory education are seen here as essentially the general or foundation stage of a longer cycle of education, which may not be completed until a student has reached his or her early twenties. In some countries, attempts have been made to develop high-level courses at the post-compulsory stage which are self-contained ("terminal"), and lead to immediate employment rather than entry to higher education. This issue is explored further in some of the case studies; in terms of Figure 1, it appears as a problem of, or ambiguity about, stages. Can such courses act at the same time as a foundation stage for higher education and a more specific stage for employment? The issue is related to the criteria used in selection in each case, which may of course vary from one faculty to another in higher education, and one occupation to another; some occupations require the very cognitive/theoretical skills that higher education also demands.

However, in many countries, the problem is that many young people do not find employment at this stage. How far does Figure 1 help us to analyse policy responses to that problem? It should first be noted that unemployment policies reflect factors that go well beyond education and training: general economic and social policies, regional differences and demographic trends constitute perhaps the main variables. In terms of education and training, much depends on the diagnosis of the problem. If youth unemployment is seen as a cyclical problem, likely to be remedied by an impending upturn in the economy, the typical reaction is to continue the existing pattern of training, to "train for stock". If on the other hand unemployment is seen as a structural problem, several policy responses may be found. There may be an attempt to upgrade the general level of the workforce, in line with the "displacement hypothesis" referred to above, or there may be shift of emphasis in terms of sectors, for example towards services. A fear of skill shortages may result in the targeting of certain occupations (such as information technology) in crash training programmes. Uncertainty about future employment trends may lead to a greater individual and policy emphasis on the general or foundation stages, which seem to "keep the options open". Preparation for self-employment is also receiving greater emphasis in some countries. And finally, the extension of initial education and training seems to be perceived in some countries partly as a substitute for, rather than preparation for, employment, whatever the stated intentions of policy-makers. In practice, many current post-compulsory policies seem to combine elements of all these responses, although there has perhaps been a general policy shift away from a "cyclical" to a "structural" diagnosis of the unemployment problem.

2. Access and responsiveness

The change from a relatively undifferentiated to a differentiated system has been explored in terms of Figure 1. In the remainder of this section, the other two themes will be briefly discussed. The first of these involves a change in the "distance" between education and society, and in the strength of the boundary between them. The stereotypical basic school, covering the first five or six years of education is a rather self-contained institution. The staff who are employed are likely to be full-time professional teachers, and although parents may play some role in the running of the institution, "outsiders" (i.e. non-teachers) typically play only a small part: coming into the school to give the occasional talk, or helping to arrange the occasional visit outside. The school is a largely distinct, self-sufficient institution, which maintains a certain distance from society. That distance is underpinned by legislation, for example in terms of the legal responsibility for the children while they are on school property and during school hours, and also indicated symbolically by restrictions, both physical and organisational, on access from the outside. The school curriculum likewise embodies an indirect or generalised relationship with the "outside world". It is typically determined by general legislation or guidelines, and is relatively unaffected by pressures from particular interest groups. The school is a world within a world, and much of the socialisation that takes place there is in fact socialisation into school *itself*, and its particular patterns and norms.

This picture is no doubt simplified, but it serves to draw a contrast with the post-compulsory stage. Institutions at that stage often pride themselves on being not distinct and self-contained, but responsive and accessible. Some of the teachers may have worked in other occupations previously, or even be part-time teachers, continuing with their other trade or profession. Even if all the teachers are full-time professionals, the curriculum will usually reflect external priorities, related to specific occupations or future studies. Both curriculum planning and institutional governance will typically involve individuals or agencies outside the education system – employers, trade unions, community leaders or representatives of special interest groups. The institution will be regarded less as a closed arena, and more of a public space, with much coming and going, and consequent problems of security. But much of the teaching and learning that occurs at the post-compulsory stage takes place outside educational institutions altogether, in the workplace, in public institutions, in libraries, in the field. Whereas at the compulsory stage all pupils are full-time, in post-compulsory education the very definition of student becomes problematic, with increasing numbers of part-time and occasional students, or students enrolling for parts of courses (modules) rather than entire programmes. In some countries, it is difficult even to draw the boundary of the education system at this stage, let alone maintain it.

Again, the picture is simplified, and does not take account of the great variety of institutional environments at this stage. Students in the traditional, pre-higher education streams are likely to experience an environment which is much more like "school" than those on technical and vocational courses, which will to some extent want to *simulate* the external work environment, and may well be partly located there. But in general terms, the post-compulsory education stage has moved into a much closer and more direct relationship with the society than is the case at the lower secondary or primary stages. It is less distant, less distinct, less self-contained, in terms of governance, staffing, curricula, access, and physical setting.

This greater proximity has several consequences for the organisation and content of studies – the focus of this report. It means that courses at this stage are much more likely to be *applied* in emphasis than before, that is, planned with reference to immediate or eventual use. This in turn creates a tension between "theory" and "practice" in many courses, in which the "internal" demands of the subject may conflict with the "external" requirements of the occupation. In fact, this tension may be less a purely epistemological one, than to do with norms and emphases, more a matter of context than content. And it takes a more general form in the conflicting policy emphases on "work-driven" and "education-driven" learning; on the culture of employment versus the culture of education. The term "culture" points to a second consequence of the reduced distance between education and society, in terms of *socialisation.* It was suggested earlier that much of the socialisation that goes on in schools is socialisation not into general social norms, but into the specific and to some extent atypical norms of school itself. By the post-compulsory stage, the pattern of socialisation has itself become more differentiated, anticipating the eventual occupations, roles and status of students. Apprentices are socialised into their particular craft or trade; technicians into the technical strata; pre-higher education students into the norms of universities. (Unemployment thus creates problems of socialisation as well as of education and training; can one, or should one, educate *for* unemployment?) None of this takes place as simply as is implied here; for one thing, peer-group and media-based cultures at this stage can exercise a powerful influence. However, the general point remains. Post-compulsory education, in all its forms, far from being the purely cognitive experience implied by some prospectuses, is heavily implicated in *affective* learning, in the formation of attitudes, values and identities. It is thus important, in any analysis of curricula at this stage, not only to consider the explicit curriculum content, but to take into account the learning process and the learning environment which may be main carriers of the affective message. This points to the significance of role models, teaching and learning methods, institutional and physical settings, and formal and informal counselling, aspects of post-compulsory education which are difficult to explore (because they are often implicit or hidden) but on which some of the case studies have a bearing.

3. Education policy and the education market

The third and last theme which helps to clarify the nature of post-compulsory education is that of the "education market". Education policy is, in the compulsory sector, largely synonymous with educational planning. This is because compulsory education is, at least in theory, plannable. Demand can only express itself in limited ways, within the parameters of compulsion. Parents can, in some systems, opt for private rather than State schools, or within the State sector, for one school rather than another. Students have some choice of subjects, or of topics within subjects, especially at the lower secondary stage. Truancy can be seen as an expression of negative demand. However, the State often has a monopoly over the supply of education, the licensing of teachers, the specification of curricula and the award of qualifications. In such circumstances, the concept of an education market makes only limited sense.

As education moves into and beyond the post-compulsory stage, however, it begins to take on some of the characteristics of a market. Demand expresses itself in decisions to enrol in one institution rather than another, on one course rather than another, indeed in the decision to enrol at all. Such demand is of course heavily influenced by pressures (from parents, peers or employers), constraints (entrance requirements) and may be "distorted" by student support policies; but most post-compulsory institutions have to keep at least one eye on recruitment. The monopoly provision of the compulsory school gives way to increasing competition among suppliers of education, including some outside the formal education system. And since the system is no longer continuous and consecutive, its output is also subject to "consumer" pressures, not only from employers, but from other parts of the system. In the latter sense, higher education is one "consumer" of post-compulsory education, and its preferences can have a significant influence on curriculum policies. Qualifications provide the main currency for this internal education market, and also link education with the external labour market.

There is still considerable scope for policy-makers to plan and regulate this education market, through legislation (for example granting legal rights to access in certain cases), administrative regulation (limiting places in certain subjects), financial strategies, accreditation of courses or institutions, and policy statements designed to influence institutional and individual choices. The extent to which governments attempt to plan this stage of education, or leave it to market forces, varies from country to country, usually in line with their broader, ideological commitment to planned or market strategies. But in general, it may be more accurate at the post-compulsory stage to regard government policy as a major, rather than determining, influence on provision; there are many policy actors involved, more than in other sectors of education.

The market metaphor should, however, be treated with some caution. To begin with, post-compulsory education and its associated employment outlets constitute not a single market, but a complex set of segmented, overlapping markets, delimited by stage, level, subject type, occupational categories, age, type of qualification, domicile and other less obvious factors such as perceived access and cultural distance. Secondly, as the Scottish case study makes clear, the pre-employment market may differ from the in-employment market. In the former, employers may be more concerned with qualifications as an indirect measure of general ability and potential (i.e. as screening devices) than as direct measures of relevant knowledge and skills (which can be instilled on the job). In the latter, however, immediate competence and low training costs may be the key criteria. The Swedish case study draws attention to the difference between low-level local labour markets, operating often on the basis of personal knowledge and contacts, and middle- and high-level national labour markets, operating on the basis of formal qualifications.

In general terms, there are problems in applying market concepts to education. Education involves many intangibles. It is difficult for students to make rational choices about courses, for teachers to make rational choices about students, and for employers to make rational choices about either. Qualifications may act as the currency of the market, but it takes a long time for employers (especially small employers) to get used to new qualifications. The benefits of education, either to the individual or society, are difficult to assess. The economic concept of equilibrium implies feedback, but the feedback mechanisms in education are tortuous and often very long-term; for example, the consequences of under-training may not appear for years or even decades (for example in construction work). The classical arguments in favour of market mechanisms cite their capacity to reconcile private good with public good. Contemporary arguments are couched more in terms of information and decision-making: markets generate more information than planners can ever have[6]. Since post-compulsory education is often described as being a jungle or a maze, this information argument deserves serious consideration and, at the very least, suggests that planners look carefully at the flow of information (in all directions) at this stage. Who knows what? How do they find out? How can the flow and quality of information be improved? Can the system be simplified without losing information? Such pragmatic advances can perhaps be made within either a planning or market orientation to general policy issues.

Post-compulsory education is a complex and confusing area of education, and the aim of this section of the report has been to try to bring about some degree of clarification. The model presented here is intended to be used as an analytic tool, not as a representation of any given system. The distinctions between different stages, sectors and levels are rarely clear-cut in practice, and operate differently in different countries. For example, the pattern in the United States is much less linear than the notion of stages would imply. As the U.S. case study notes: "Few decisions are irreversible. People may leave education and return later, not once, but several times over a lifetime, to complete "unfinished business" such as to receive a high school diploma or its equivalent". Some European systems, by contrast, are more clearly organised in stages. The concepts of economic sector and cognitive level are equally problematic. Increasingly, labour market analysis is directed less at broad employment sector groupings, than at occupational categories, or at problems and developments which cut across the traditional sector boundaries. As regards the notion of level, it should be pointed out that in some countries, such as Germany and Switzerland, vocational education and training have their own kind of status, which is widely regarded as being different from, rather than lower than, general courses, and which attracts many very able students. Indeed, the idea of a plurality of types, rather than levels of ability, will emerge as an important theme in the report.

Despite these caveats, the analysis in this section should help to place the case studies in perspective, in two ways. First, it permits a clearer understanding of terms and labels. The case studies took as their point of departure the division of post-compulsory education into "general", "technical", and "vocational" types or streams, which had emerged from previous OECD studies. One of the main aims of this study was to discover how far these demarcations still existed. Figure 2 relates this tripartite division to the model in Figure 1, defining each type or stream in terms of stage, sector and level. "General" programmes or streams refer mainly to the general or foundation stage of long-cycle education, leading to high-level employment in all sectors, usually through higher education. Such streams tend to be dominated by the need to lay a foundation for access to higher education, and typically lead to a well-established upper secondary certificate. (In the United States, such streams are called academic or pre-academic; the "general" streams are relatively less prestigious.) "Technical" streams exist more clearly in some countries than others; where they do, they typically comprise the foundation stage of a middle-length educational cycle leading to intermediate occupations in all sectors. Technical streams, like general ones, tend to be full-time, though they may involve practical placements, and historically were associated mainly with the secondary (manufacturing) sector. "Vocational" streams typically refer to the foundation or even specific stage of a short educational cycle, leading to ready competence in some craft or skilled occupation. Such streams may be mainly school-based or work-based, or involve a combination of each in a "dual" system; and they are sometimes therefore classified (misleadingly in terms of the learning process) as part-time. More recently, "vocational" streams have become much more heterogeneous and therefore more difficult to characterise in terms of stage, sector or level. Some of them represent a broad foundation for a family of occupations, while others are geared to a specific and well-defined type of work; many of them are now oriented towards service sector occupations, rather than their traditional outlets in manufacturing industries. The range of abilities has also become wider, driven up on the one hand by labour market competition and the increasing cognitive and theoretical demands of technology, and lowered on the other by the inclusion of remedial courses for those who are regarded as being at risk in

Figure 2. **THE OECD TYPOLOGY**

Stream	Educational stage	Economic sector	Cognitive level
General	General/ foundation	All	High
Technical	Foundation	Originally secondary; now all	Middle
Vocational	Foundation/ specific	Originally secondary; now all	Middle Low Remedial

educational, employment or broader social terms. The form or format of vocational programmes has grown correspondingly diverse, with the introduction of innovative methods for those who would reject more traditional forms of teaching and training.

Two problems with Figure 2 should be noted. The first is the potential confusion between "general" used to describe the first stage in an educational cycle, and "general" used to refer to a particular stream (pre-academic in Europe, but not in the United States, and rather broader in Japan). The second, and more important, is the existence of courses which cut across the categories in the diagram. Examples of "grey areas" between streams appear in a number of the studies, for example the Italian and Swedish. In some countries, some programmes are described as "all-ability", the essential differentiation being in the sector orientation rather than level or stage of work. It is difficult to distinguish between the "technical" and the "vocational" in the Swiss system. This is also partly the case with the Yugoslav system, and with the Technical and Vocational Education Initiative (TVEI) in the United Kingdom. Whether such programmes do in fact recruit right across the ability spectrum can only be established by a detailed analysis of enrolments and destinations, and where such programmes are recent, such data are not yet available. However, it is worth making the point that some systems are not as segmented or stratified, in intention or reality, as Figure 2 suggests.

Figures 1 and 2 provide only a *point of departure* for the report. The analysis that follows will show how each of the three dimensions in the diagrams has to be modified in the light of current developments, and the pattern that eventually emerges will be more complex and more fluid. First, however, it is necessary to give a brief descriptive and quantitative picture of structures and trends in the eleven systems.

III

STRUCTURES AND TRENDS

Before describing the findings of the case studies in the eleven countries, it is necessary to place them in some kind of quantitative and structural perspective. This chapter will therefore attempt to set out the broad similarities and differences between countries as regards structures and trends in post-compulsory education and training, drawing mainly on OECD data. More detailed information, in particular that related to the main theme of this study is available in some of the country reports. This chapter is divided into three sections: The first presents some of the contextual variables in demography and employment which affect policies in this sector of education; the second describes the education and training structures in each country; the third presents available data within OECD which reflect different forms of provision at the post-compulsory level.

1. Contextual trends

Post-compulsory education is affected by a number of contextual factors which lie outside the education system itself. Three of these are of particular importance to this study: demographic trends; trends in the distribution of employment between economic sectors; and trends in unemployment, especially youth unemployment. These will be examined briefly in turn.

The crude birth rates for ten countries are displayed in Figure 3. In all cases the general trend from 1965 to 1970 is downward, though the steepness of the descent varies and in some cases there is some indication of a levelling out. Assuming that, in most cases, the post-compulsory stage begins at about the age of sixteen, it is clear that the size of the cohorts typically enrolling at this level is decreasing and will continue to do so in the foreseeable future. One cannot simply translate demographic trends into enrolment trends, because of the factors which affect demand at the post-compulsory stage, but in general it would appear that systems are facing either contraction or at best stabilisation at a lower level than previously. This might have several effects. It could begin to ease problems of youth unemployment, as smaller cohorts begin to arrive on the labour market; indeed in the medium term it could pose problems of labour shortages in countries such as Germany where the demographic decline is marked. It could lead to the rationalisation of existing provision, with closure or merging of institutions, and conflation of previously distinct lines or streams of study. It could lead to increased competition among providers for students in a contracting market. It could result in

Figure 3. **CRUDE BIRTH RATES**
Per thousand

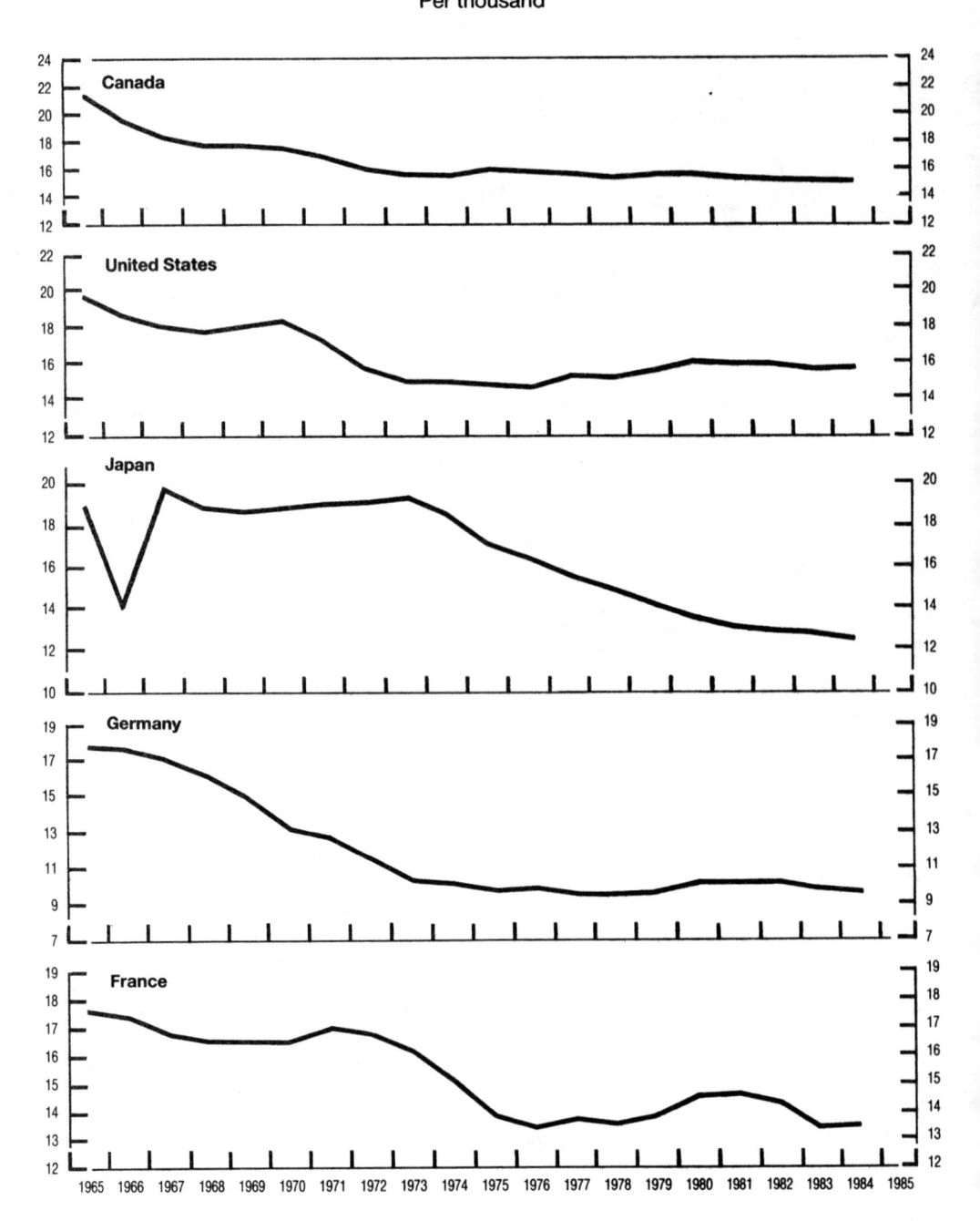

Source: OECD Demographic Data Bank.

Figure 3 (Contd.)

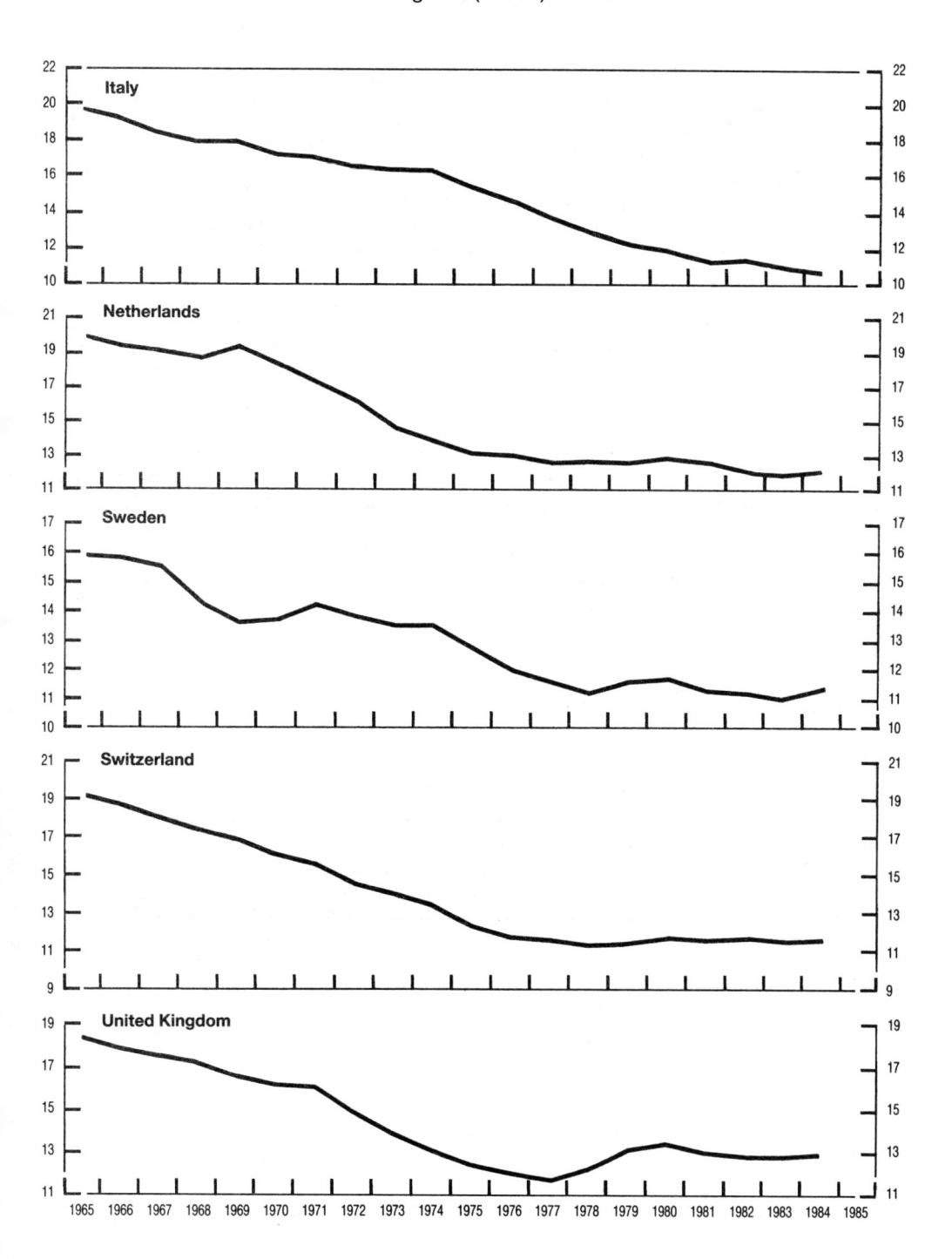

post-compulsory education institutions in some countries becoming less age-specific in an attempt to tap alternative, and in some cases, growing adult markets, bringing a shift of emphasis from "tertiary" to "community". Aggregate birth rate trends, however, may conceal considerable variations in component trends, for example in the birth rate in different social classes, or among different ethnic groups. To the extent that particular streams or types of post-compulsory education are linked to particular types of intake, such variations matter. It is possible for shortages in particular types of courses, and their related "levels" of occupation, to coexist with adequate or surplus intakes in others.

The second main contextual variable is the distribution of employment among the three main economic sectors, and in particular the trend towards the tertiary sector mentioned in the previous chapter. Table 1 gives the employment trends in the three sectors in relevant countries over the last 20 years; a long time series here is necessary in order to observe structural changes. While the figures vary from country to country, the general trend is clear. For all OECD countries, the proportion of the civilian labour force employed in the primary sector has fallen from over 17 per cent in 1965 to 9 in 1984; the proportion employed in the secondary sector has decreased less sharply from just over a third of the workforce to just under (with a countervailing trend in Japan helping to mask larger falls in North American and European countries); and the percentage employed in the tertiary sector has grown from 46 per cent in 1965 to about 60 per cent in 1984. Indeed the service sector accounts for over two-thirds of all civilian employment in 5 out of the 24 ountries, with several others approaching that proportion. The importance of the long-term trend towards the tertiary sector thus seems clear. It may be that this will continue, though the consequences for the balance of payments of a continuing decline in manufacturing may affect it in some countries. It should also be remembered that, from the point of view of education and training, the service sector is by no means a homogeneous category, and the implications for education are far from straightforward.

Table 1
CIVILIAN EMPLOYMENT BY SECTOR
In percentages (rounded)

	1965			1975			1984		
	Primary	Secondary	Tertiary	Primary	Secondary	Tertiary	Primary	Secondary	Tertiary
Canada	10	33	57	6	29	65	5	26	69
United States	6	36	58	4	31	65	3	29	68
Japan	24	32	44	13	36	52	9	35	56
France	18	39	43	10	39	51	8	33	59
Germany	11	48	41	7	45	48	6	41	53
Italy	26	37	37	17	39	44	12	35	54
Netherlands	8	41	51	6	35	59	5	27	68
Sweden	11	43	46	6	37	57	5	30	65
Switzerland	11	48	41	8	42	50	7	38	56
United Kingdom	4	47	50	3	41	57	3	33	65
OECD average	17	37	46	12	35	54	9	31	60

Source: OECD, *Labour Force Statistics 1964-1984*, Paris, July 1986.

The third contextual variable which affects post-compulsory education is youth unemployment. It is important here not only to consider actual unemployment among the post-compulsory age group, but the prospect of unemployment in the years that immediately follow, since this may affect both students' perception of the problem and the education systems' response. Table 2 gives unemployment trends for the under 24 age group in ten of the case study countries over the decade 1975-1985, together with the peak year. With the exception of the United States, the trend has been up in all countries, doubling or trebling in France, Italy, Netherlands and the United Kingdom. However, all the countries, except two, experienced their peak year between 1982 and 1984, indicating that the worst may be over, although such trends are contingent upon general economic variables, and are also in some cases affected by the introduction of special employment or training measures for the age group. The general implication of the figures is however clear. In the great majority of OECD countries, this stage of education which has traditionally used prospective employment as a basis for curriculum planning has had that basis partly removed.

Table 2
YOUTH UNEMPLOYMENT 1975-1985
Males and females under age 24 (percentages)

	1975	1980	1985	Peak year
Canada	12.0	13.2	16.5	1983
United States	15.2	13.3	13.0	1982
Japan	3.1	3.4	4.8	1984
France	7.9	15.0	25.6	1985
Germany	5.2	3.9	9.5	1985
Italy	12.8	25.2	33.4	1985
Netherlands	5.2	7.2	23.5	1984
Sweden	3.8	5.1	5.8	1983
Switzerland	0.7	0.2	0.9	1984
United Kingdom	8.6	14.1	21.7	1983

Sources: OECD, *Labour Force Statistics 1964-1984*, July 1986, except Switzerland (OFIAMT, Bern).

2. Structures

The structure of education and training at the post-compulsory stage is often complex and difficult to grasp in one country, let alone eleven. Indeed it has been referred to in some countries as a "jungle" or a "maze". It may be useful therefore to show the structure in each of the countries in a standardized, diagrammatic form, both in order to illustrate the differences between the various structures, and to provide an aid to interpreting the case studies in the next section. Diagrams 1 to 12 give the structures for twelve countries between approximately the ages of 12 and 21, so that the post-compulsory stage can be seen in relation to what goes before it and what comes after. In each case, the "theoretical" age of the student is given in the left margin, "theoretical" because it can vary according to the exact date of the student's birthday, and the extent to which he or she repeats years of study. Clear boxes in the diagrams indicate "general" type courses, while shaded boxes indicate technical/vocational. Lined boxes indicate part-time study, often in conjunction with work-based training or apprenticeship. The arrows indicate the main, though not only, routes of progression through the system. The labels given to the various institutions and types of course have been to some extent standardised to facilitate comparison. The diagrams are inevitably simplified, and cannot hope to indicate all the precise divisions and relationships between the various elements in the system. They show only the main pattern for each country, a point that should be remembered particularly in the case of countries with federal or regional variations, such as Canada, Germany, Switzerland and Yugoslavia, and in this respect, the United Kingdom. In many countries, changes in the main pattern are either being implemented or contemplated.

Detailed comments on the structures are given in some of the case studies, and in some of the more recent OECD reviews of national policy. Here there is only room to make a few general points. First, it is clear that major differences exist at the preceding, lower-secondary stage, with comprehensive systems in the majority of the countries contrasting with the more differentiated ones in France, Germany and the Netherlands. However, the lower compulsory limit in Italy and Yugoslavia mean that those systems are in some ways similar to the more differentiated ones, and even in comprehensive systems, there may be well-defined curricular streams or tracks within the common institution. At the post-compulsory stage itself, some systems appear to be more complex than others, but it should be remembered that systems which are institutionally homogeneous may nevertheless be complex and heterogeneous in terms of curricula and qualifications – dimensions that do not appear in the diagrams. Nevertheless, a great diversity of patterns is evident: in some involving a strong emphasis on part-time or even correspondence education, in others showing many horizontal routes for progression as well as the more obvious vertical ones. There is less diversity at the higher education level, reflecting the key role of the university.

Two general observations about these diagrams can be made. First, they induce caution about making cross-national comparisons. If the post-compulsory stage is the most complex stage in each system, that complexity is compounded once one begins to compare, and the diagrams only begin to illustrate the complexity. Comparative studies of this particular stage are thus perhaps uniquely difficult to make, and probably to read. But there may be a more positive point. The diversity of structures suggests the need to concentrate on *functions*. What each system does may be more important than the exact way it does it; after all, there may be various educational means of attaining the same educational end. The means will reflect the contingencies of history, society and policy. The ends are likely to be similar in all countries which have reached a similar stage of economic development; although that should not be taken to imply a simple economic determinism. The emphasis on functions rather than structures should, however, allow a more fruitful interpretation of the case studies, and point the way towards some more general conclusions.

Diagram 1. **CANADA**

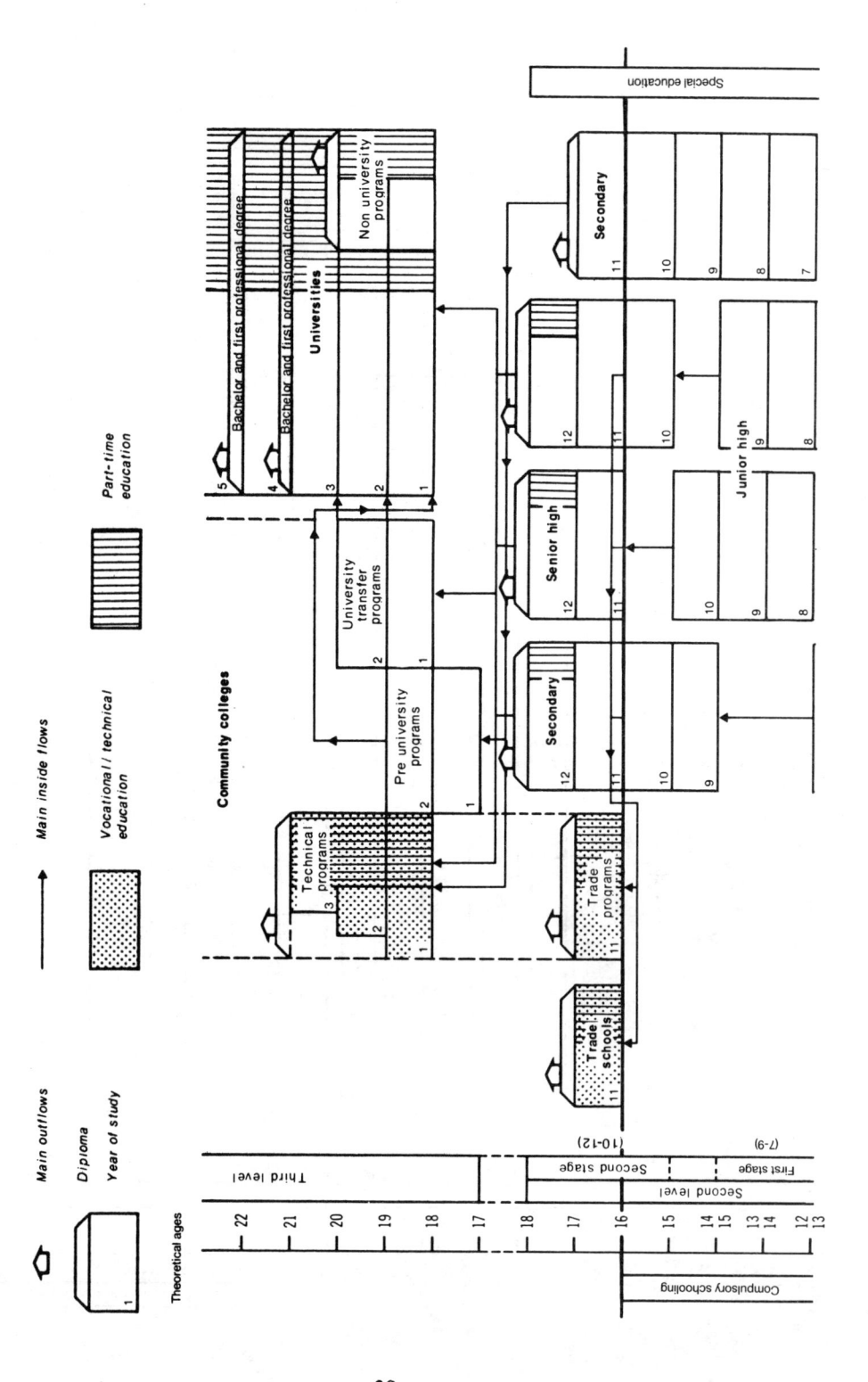

Diagram 2. **FRANCE**

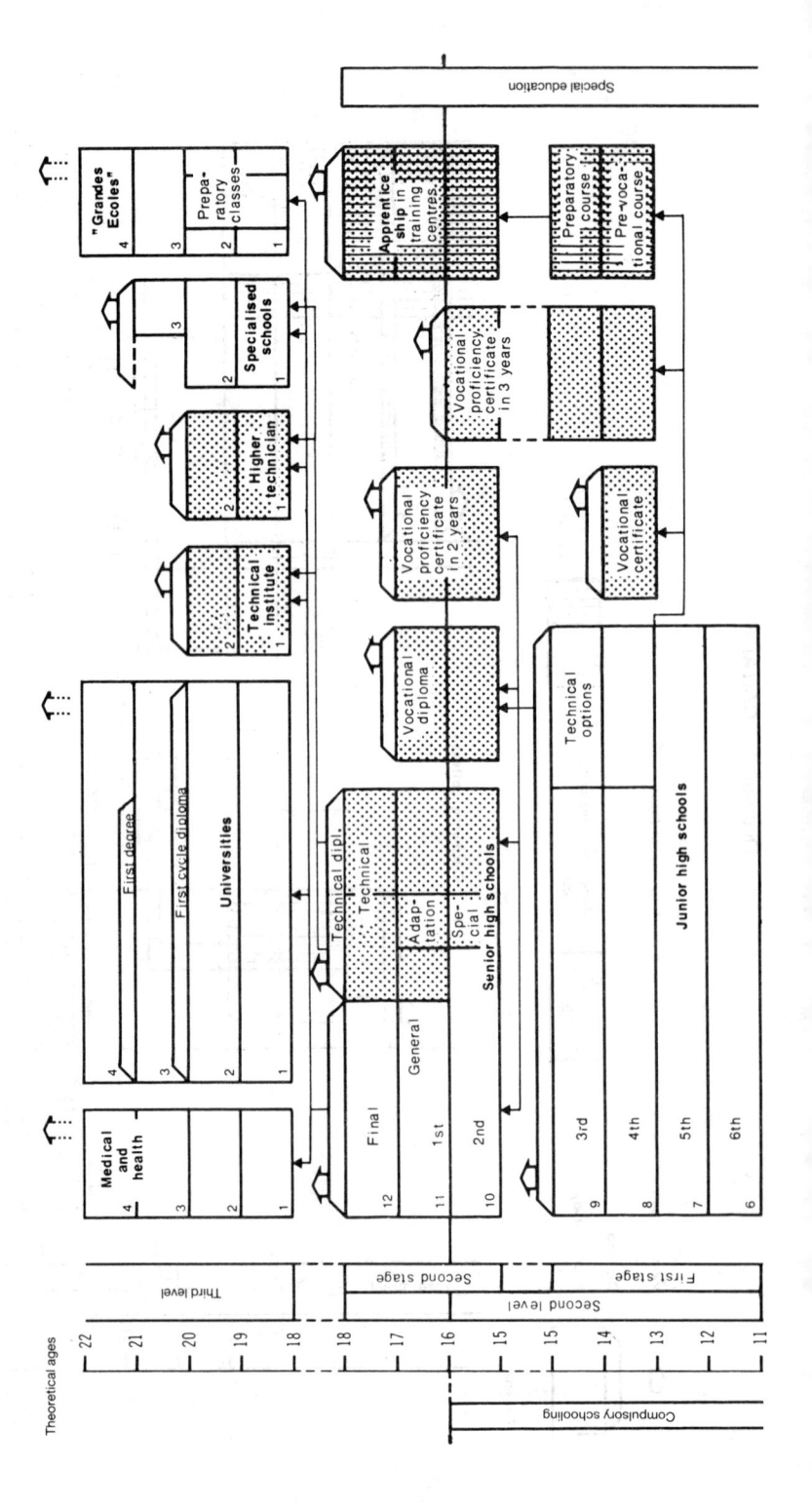

Diagram 3. **GERMANY**

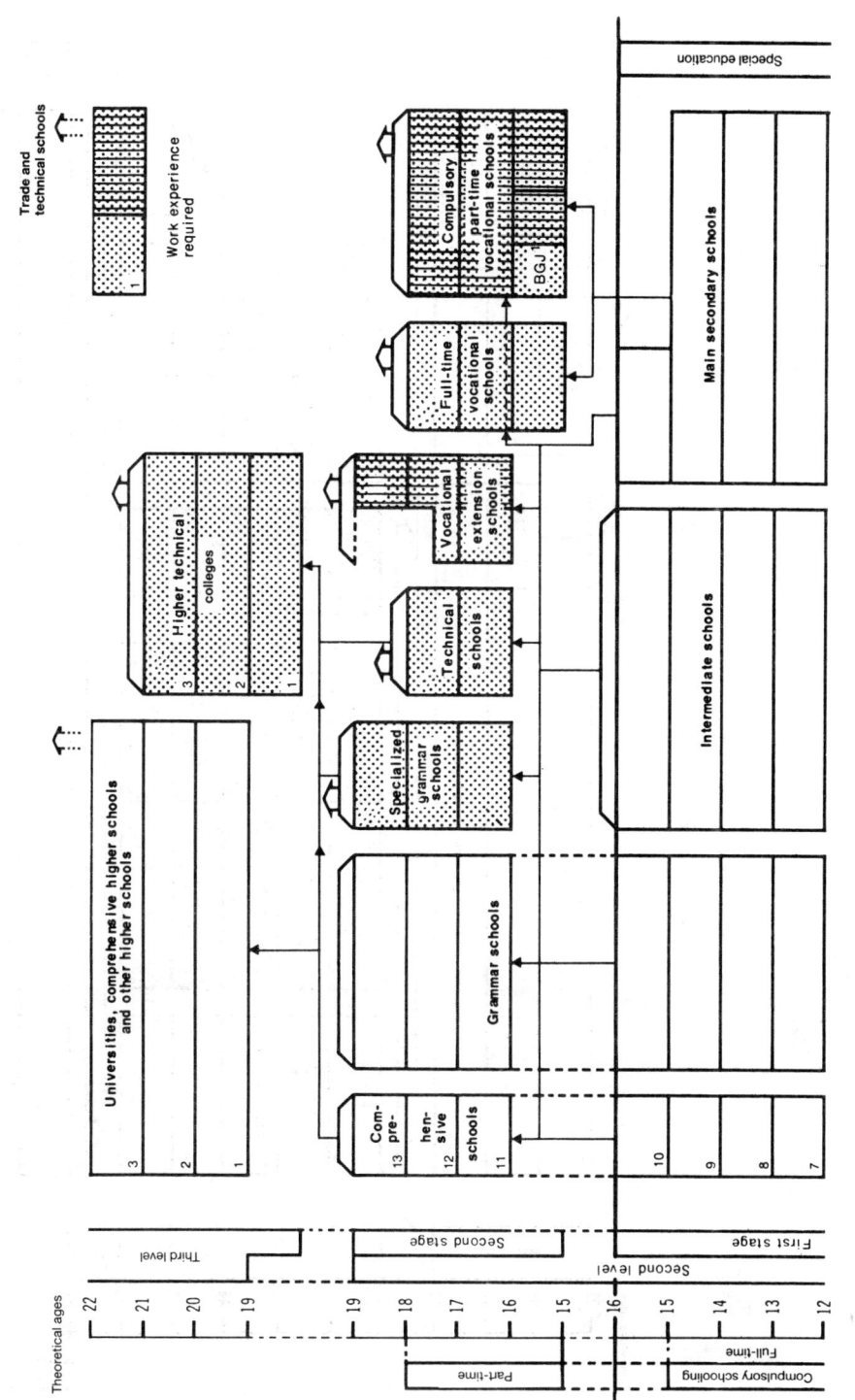

Diagram 4. **ITALY**

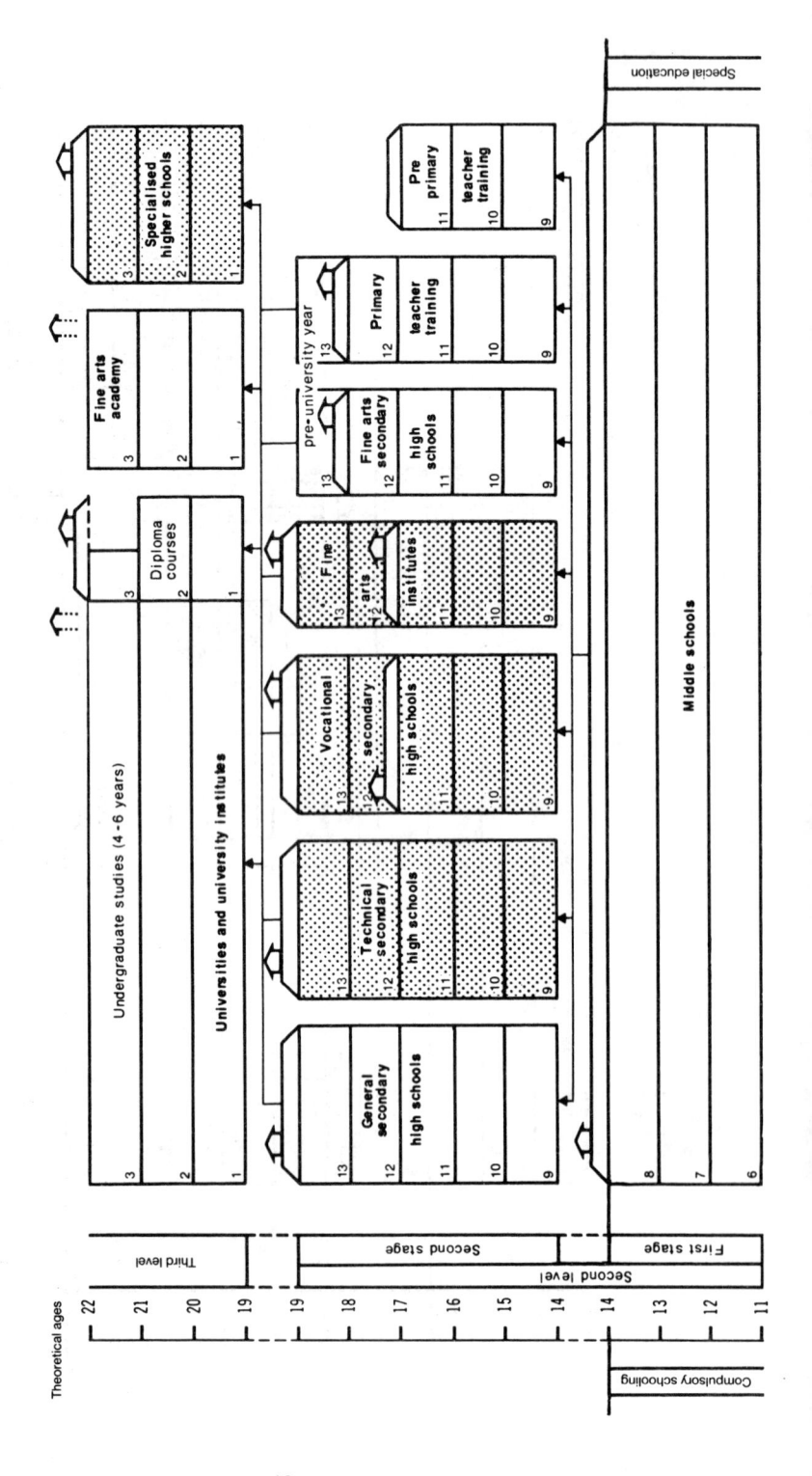

Diagram 5. JAPAN

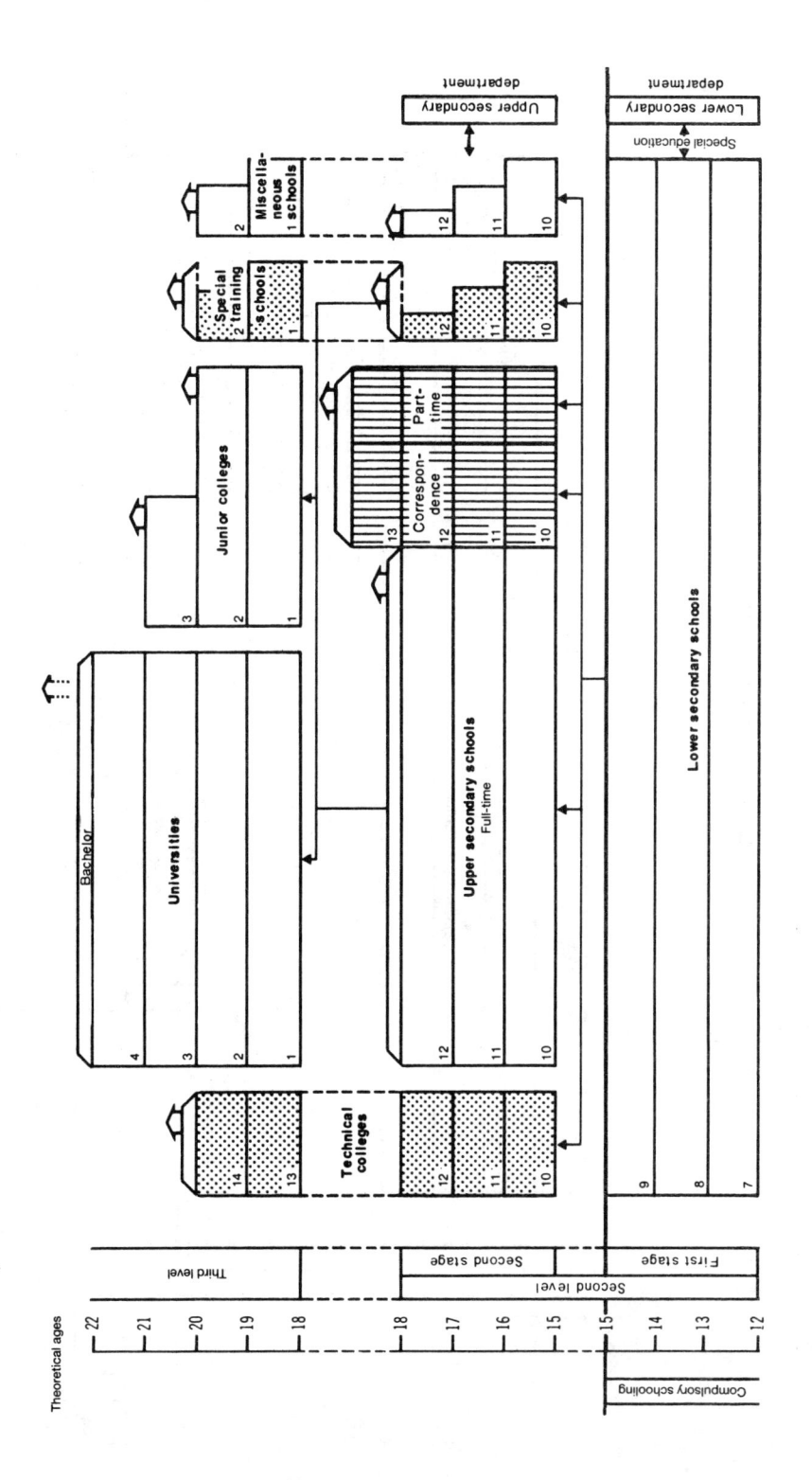

Diagram 6. **NETHERLANDS**

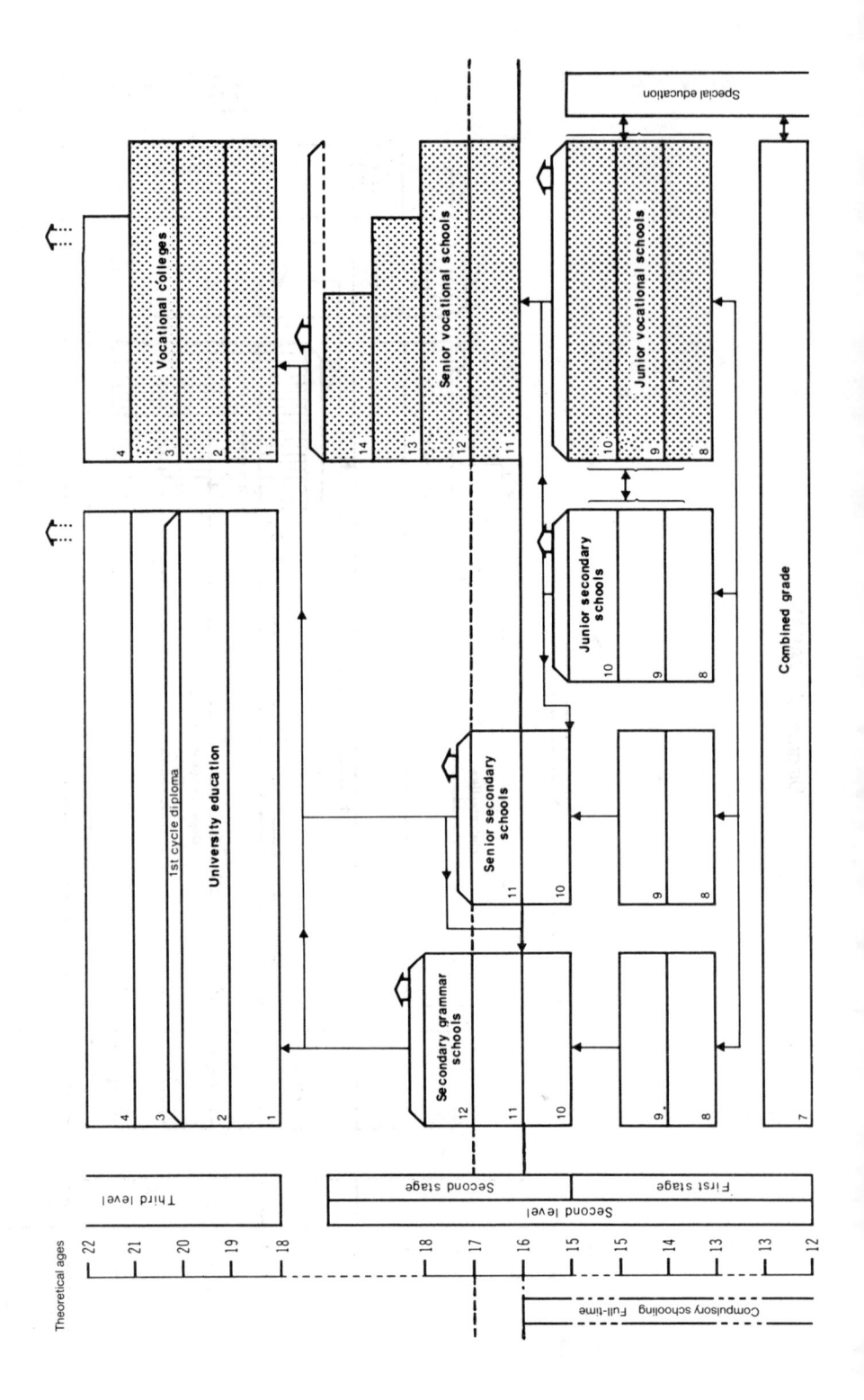

Diagram 7. **SWEDEN**

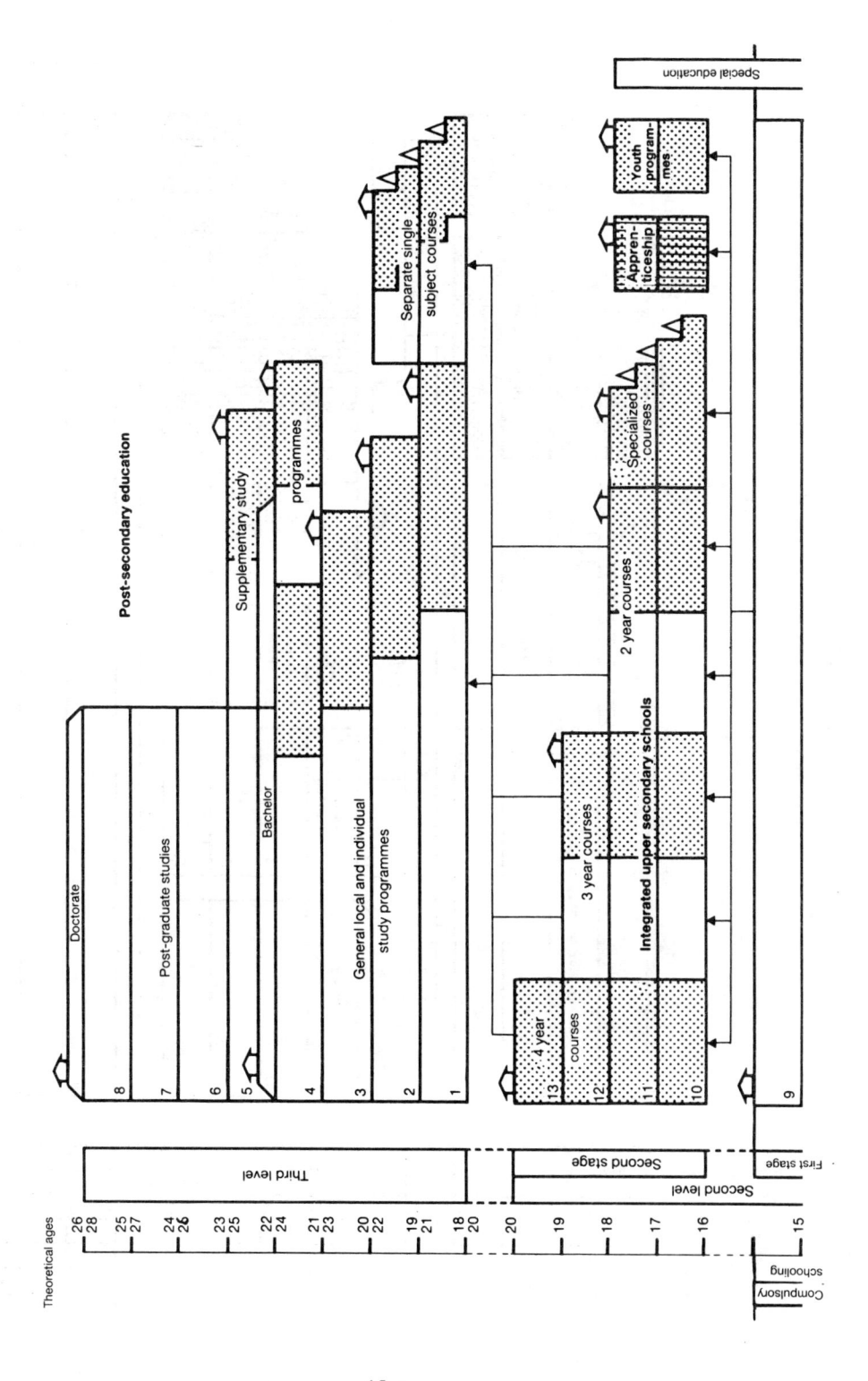

Diagram 8. **SWITZERLAND**

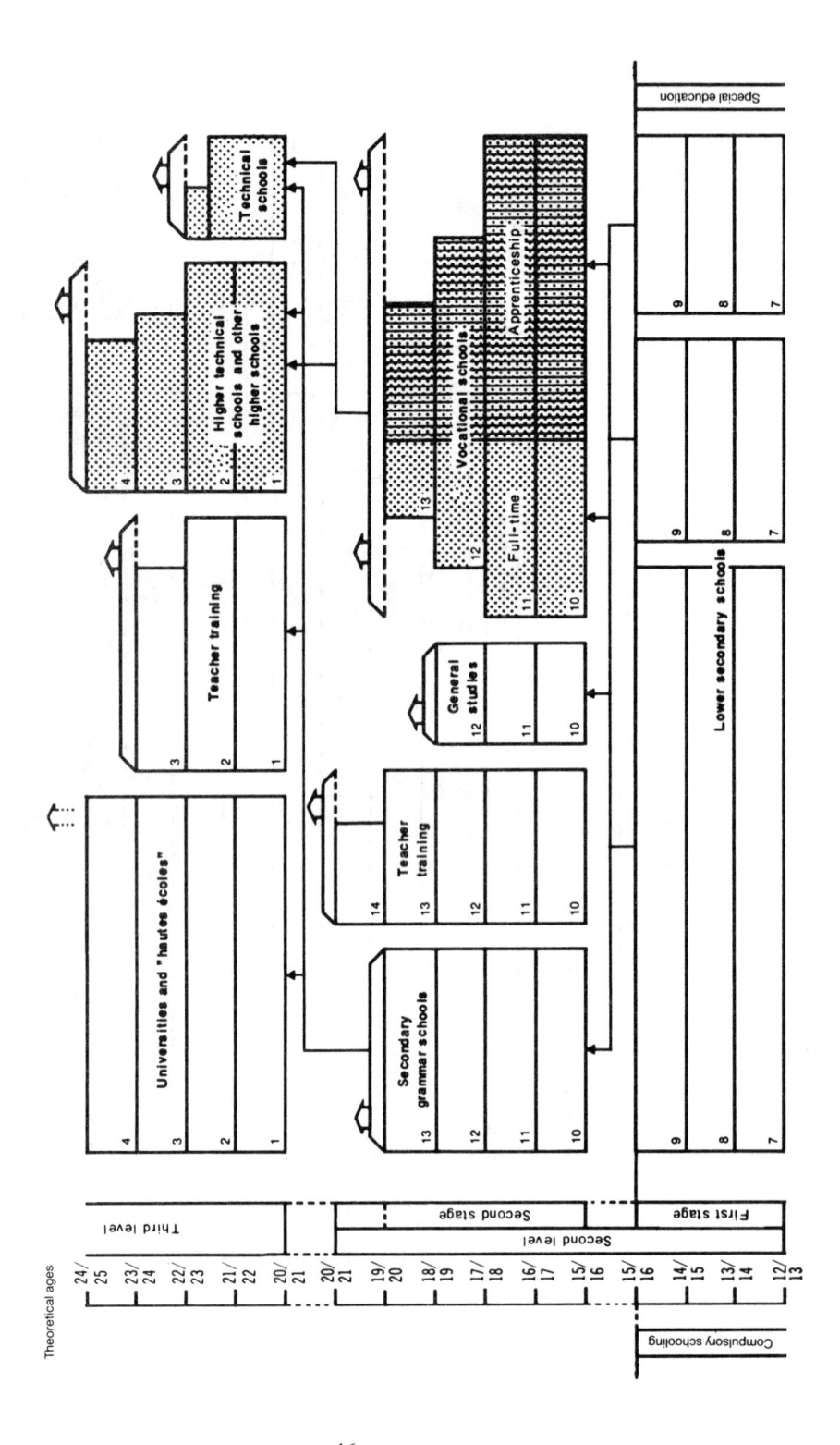

Diagram 9. **UNITED KINGDOM (ENGLAND AND WALES)**

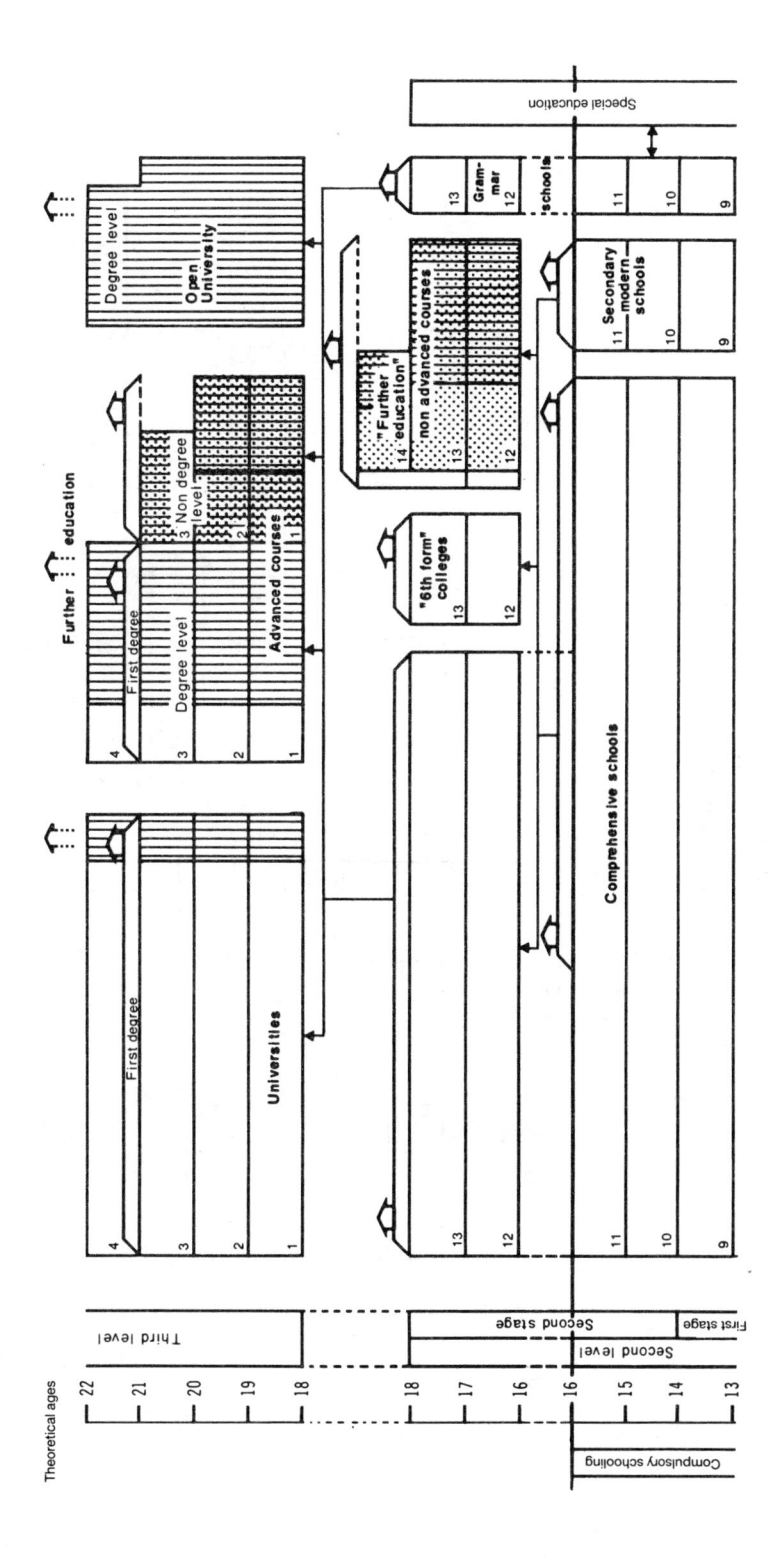

Diagram 10. **UNITED KINGDOM (SCOTLAND)**

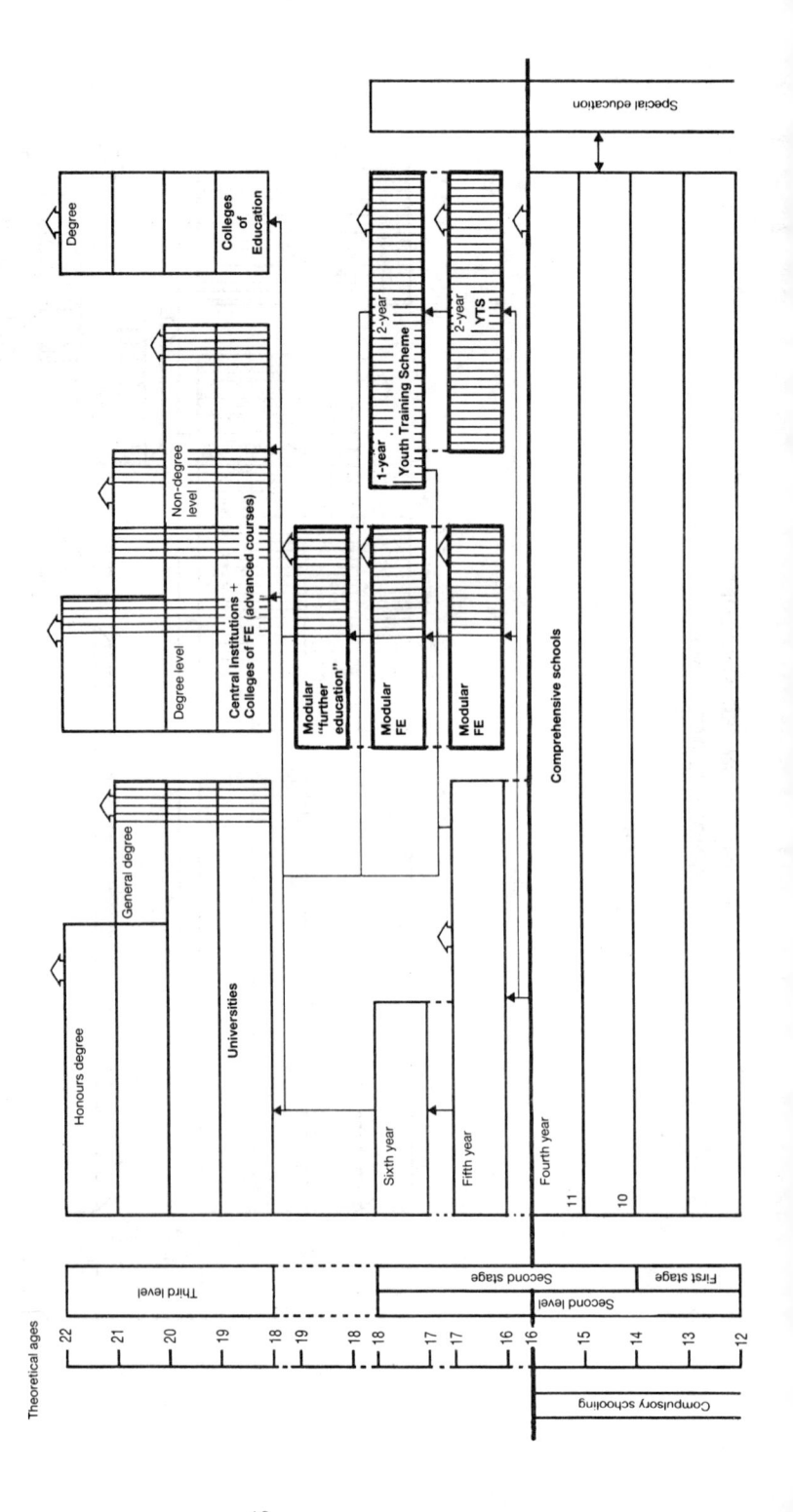

Diagram 11. **UNITED STATES**

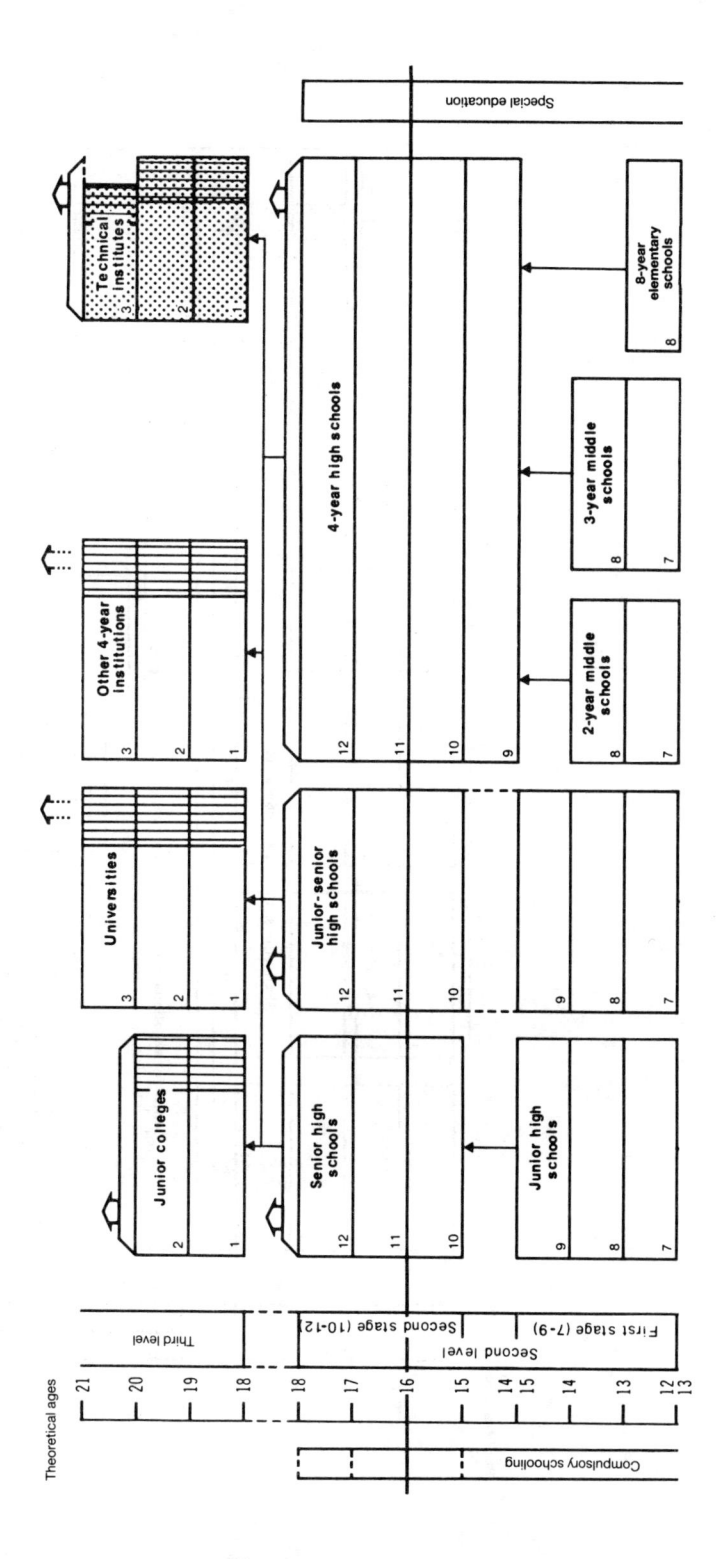

Diagram 12. **YUGOSLAVIA**

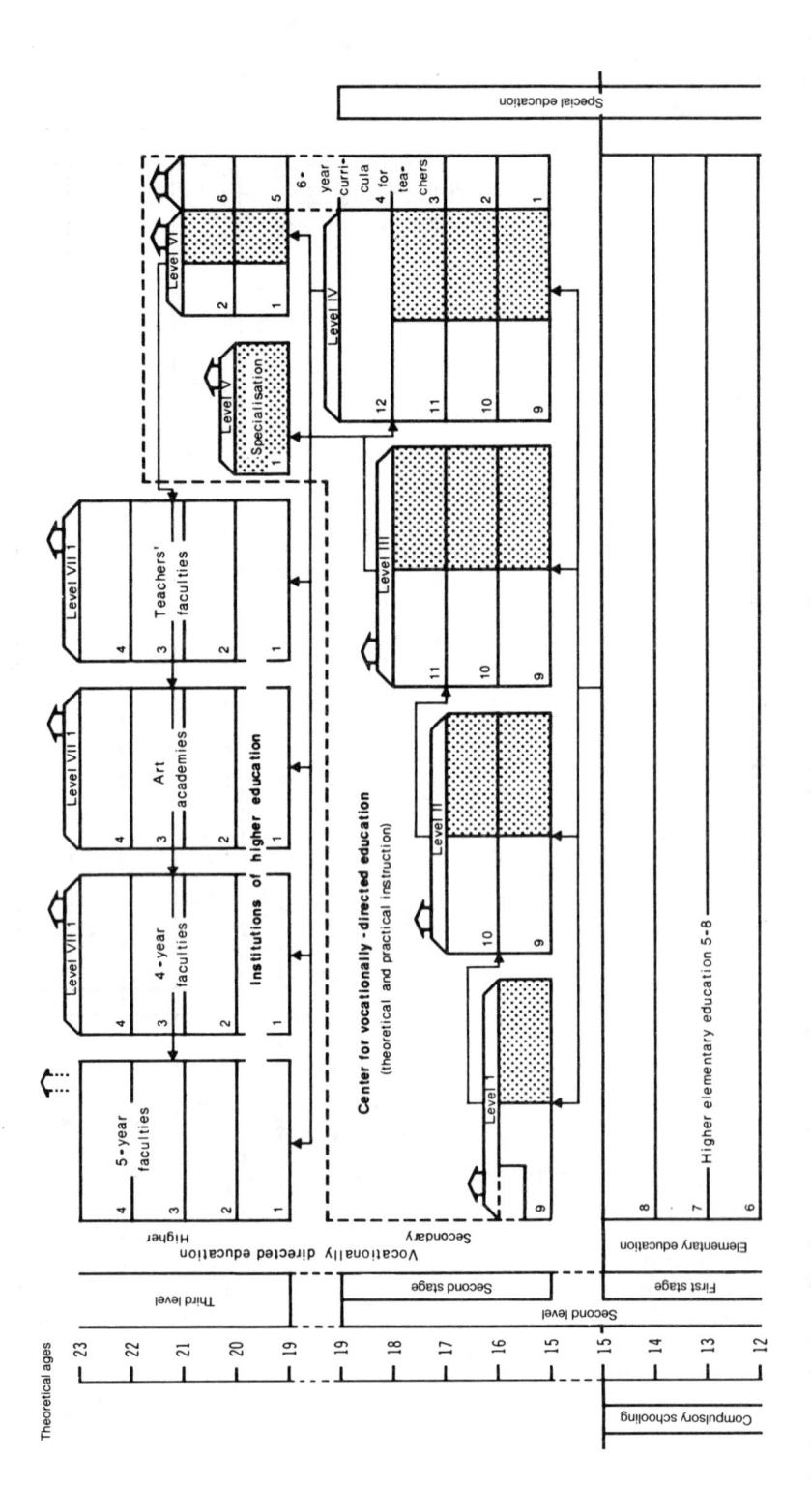

3. Educational and training trends

In order to understand how different post-compulsory education systems actually work, it would greatly help if one could relate statistical trends to the structures shown in the preceding diagrams of each system. Actual numbers or percentages within each box in the diagram would have allowed to see the relative importance of each element in the structure and flows of students between them. The notional 100 per cent enrolments of the compulsory sector could thus be traced, through the various pathways of the post-compulsory stage, to their first destinations in the labour market and perhaps even beyond. However, since such data are not generally available, and even when they are, they cannot easily form the basis for cross national comparisons, only aggregate, and more static measures can be presented here.

Table 3
DISTRIBUTION OF PUPILS IN UPPER
SECONDARY EDUCATION 1984/85
Percentage

	General	Technical/ vocational	Total	Part-time
Canada	–	–	100	–
France	31.1	55.0	86.1	13.9
Germany	19.6	17.2	36.8	63.2
Italy	22.2	77.8	100	–
Japan	66.0	30.4	96.4	3.6
Netherlands	45.0	55.0	100	–
Sweden	22.7	77.3	100	–
Switzerland	17.9	6.6	24.5	75.5
United Kingdom	56.5	9.2	65.7	34.3
United States	–	–	100	–
Yugoslavia	40.7	59.3	100	–

Source: OECD Educational Data Bank.

Table 3 shows the structural differences among education systems at the upper secondary level. Unfortunately the classification adopted in the OECD statistics does not exactly correspond to the one used in this study: general, technical, vocational. In the OECD classification, no distinction is made between different lines of study within general education, although it is known that these often lead to different types and levels of occupations. The large proportions of students in general education both in Quebec (Table 3a) and the United States (Table 3b) do not reflect the variety of choices actually available to young people in these systems. Enrolments in full-time technical and vocational education are grouped together since in some countries it is not possible to make such a distinction. Part-time education refers mainly to vocational training and apprenticeship which provides a combined school-enterprise training. It could therefore be classified in the present study as "vocational".

Table 3 *a*

QUEBEC – EVOLUTION OF THE DISTRIBUTION OF
REGULAR STUDENTS ENROLLED
IN THE CEGEPs BY TYPE OF STUDY

Percentage

	1971/72	1985/86
General (pre-university)	56.3	51.7
Technical	43.7	48.3

Note: Given the large number of adults enrolled in the CEGEPs it can be assumed that the proportion of enrolments in general pre-university courses would be larger if only the 16-19 year group were taken into account.
Source: Case study: Quebec (OECD Educational Monographs, 1987).

Table 3 *b*

UNITED STATES – PERCENT OF HIGH SCHOOL SENIORS
IN ACADEMIC GENERAL AND
VOCATIONAL PROGRAMMES BY SEX, 1972-1980

Program	All Seniors 1972	All Seniors 1980	Male 1972	Male 1980	Female 1972	Female 1980
Total	100.0	100.0	100.0	100.0	100.0	100.0
Academic	46.1	38.0	48.7	39.0	43.5	38.4
General	31.7	37.2	33.0	38.0	30.4	35.9
Vocational	22.2	24.8	18.3	23.0	26.1	25.7

Source: Fetters *et al.* (1984), Table 2.1 (included in the Country study: United States, p. 93, 1987).

Bearing in mind these problems of taxonomy, it is possible to classify Member countries – whether or not they have been included in this study – in three broad categories. The first includes those countries where the majority of enrolled young people are in full-time general education. Table 3 shows that this is clearly the case in Japan and the United Kingdom. Figures included in the Quebec study on the CEGEPs (Table 3a) and in the United States report (Table 3b) also allow for their inclusion in this category. The second category includes those countries where full-time technical/vocational programmes recruit a relatively high proportion of the student body: France, Italy, the Netherlands, Sweden and Yugoslavia. In the third group of countries, typically those with dual systems such as Germany and Switzerland, part-time schooling – mainly vocational – is the predominant pattern of studies. It should be stressed however that these tables do not include a range of full-time and part-time programmes for young people that in many countries are provided outside the formal school system and are not included in the OECD statistics from which these tables are drawn. Nevertheless, the analysis in the next chapter will show that the curriculum map of post-compulsory education varies less from country to country than the institutional map.

Gender differences in the choice of post-compulsory studies are shown in Table 4, giving the percentage of female students in each broad type of programme. Young women are

Table 4

PERCENTAGE OF GIRLS
IN DIFFERENT TYPES OF UPPER
SECONDARY EDUCATION, 1984/85

	Full-time General	Full-time Technical/vocational	Full-time Total	Part-time
Canada	–	–	44.8	–
France	58.5	47.9	52.3	26.3
Germany	50.1	54.9	52.4	41.1
Italy	53.2	48.5	49.7	–
Japan	51.0	45.2	49.3	32.3
Netherlands	51.4	46.1	48.6	–
Sweden	63.7	52.2	55.4	–
Switzerland	50.9	66.9	56.6	37.2
United Kingdom	49.2	54.7	50.1	51.1
United States	–	–	48.9	–
Yugoslavia	47.7	45.9	46.7	–

Source: OECD Educational Data Bank.

over-represented in full-time education in five of the eleven countries listed, particularly in the case of Sweden and Switzerland. In seven out of the nine countries where it was possible to distinguish between full-time general and full-time technical/vocational education, female students represent more than half of the student body in general lines of study; in four, they exceed 50 per cent in the technical/vocational sector. In most countries the highest concentration of women is found in general education; the exceptions are Germany, Switzerland and the United Kingdom, all countries where part-time studies are strongly developed. Finally, with the exception of the United Kingdom, female students are under-represented in part-time, mainly vocational programmes, reflecting perhaps the male traditions of apprenticeship.

Differences among countries both in terms of the structure of their post-compulsory systems and student participation by sex are also illustrated in Figure 4 showing the distribution of 17 year-old male and female students in the different types of programmes. The advantage of focusing on the 17 year-olds is that it allows one to control certain structural differences; indeed it is the only age group which in practically all Member countries is typically enrolled at the upper secondary level; in some countries 16 year-olds are still in compulsory schooling whereas in others, a relatively high percentage of 18 year-olds are in post-secondary education. Available data only allow the inclusion of figures for eight countries and even for some of them the information is incomplete: 21 to 42 per cent of young male students and 29 to 48 per cent of young female students at this age enrol in general education. The proportion exceeds 50 per cent only in the United Kingdom and, again, only in the case of girls. Far greater differences among countries are found in the area of full-time technical/vocational education: from 13 to 52 per cent of young women and an even wider range of young men, ranging from 5 to 57 per cent. France and the Netherlands have the highest concentration of 17 year-old students in full-time technical/vocational education. Part-time study programmes recruit from 20 to 74 per cent of 17 year-old boys and from 5 to 58 per cent of girls of the same age. For both sexes this is by far the dominant sector in

Figure 4. DISTRIBUTION OF 17 YEAR-OLD MALE AND FEMALE STUDENTS AT THE UPPER SECONDARY LEVEL BY TYPES OF PROGRAMMES, 1984/85

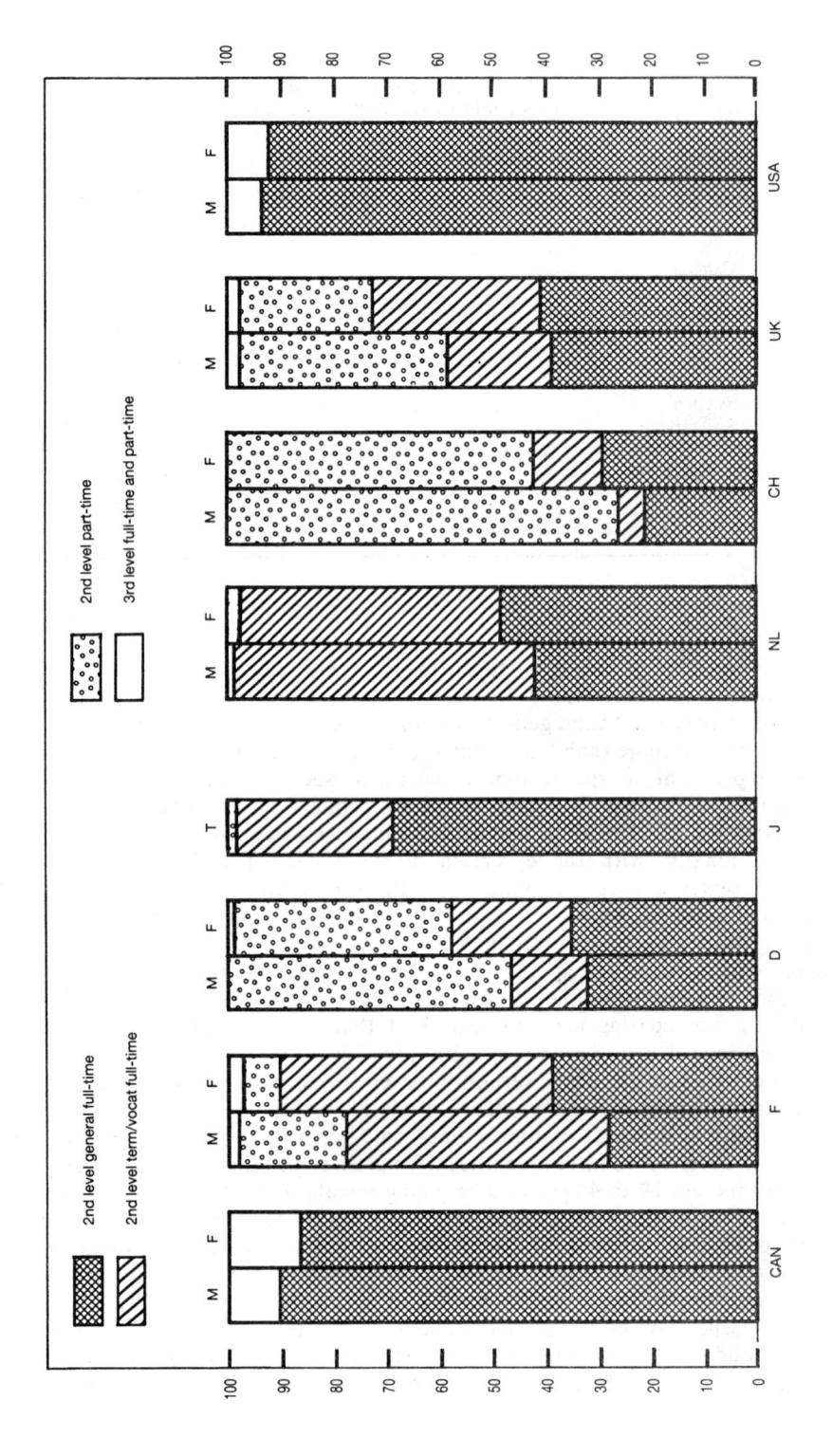

Source: OECD Educational Data Bank.

Germany and Switzerland and also, although to a lesser extent, for young male students in the United Kingdom. Finally, although in general only a very small proportion of this age group is already enrolled in post-secondary education, in the case of Canada (e.g. CEGEPs) and the United States, the percentage is far from negligible. Except for Switzerland and the United Kingdom 17 year-old girls are better represented at the post secondary level than their male counterparts. Since young women most often enrol in full-time studies, particularly in general education courses which do not prepare directly for a job, it is not surprising that they proceed to higher education at a relatively younger age than young men.

Also of interest in the context of this study are the actual participation rates in education and training (including all levels of education) of the 16-19 year age group. Table 5 provides this global information for a few countries in 1984/85. Figures should be interpreted with caution since they do not include all types of training provided outside the formal education sector. Nevertheless, what the table does indicate is that even though this stage of education is no longer compulsory in most countries, it generally enrols about two-thirds of the age group, and in some case-study countries, around three-quarters. It is interesting to note the high figures registered in Germany and in Switzerland which are above those of the United States. Although it may be claimed that the high participation rates in these two countries are largely due to the large proportion of young people who attend vocational schools on a part-time basis, it should be noted that they do, in fact, receive a *full-time* training, part of which takes place at school and part within the enterprise.

Table 5
ENROLMENT RATES IN FORMAL EDUCATION
OF THE 16-19 YEAR AGE GROUP,
1984/85

Canada	63
France	62
Germany	82
Netherlands	66
Switzerland	74
United Kingdom	38
United States	71

Source: OECD Educational Data Bank.

Figure 5 showing enrolment rates by level and modes of attendance (full-time and part-time in the case of upper secondary education) provides a better basis for a comparative analysis in that it reflects more clearly how different systems of provision affect participation rates in each country. With the exception of the United Kingdom, the participation rates of the 16 year-olds are in general very high – above 85 per cent. In Germany one quarter and in Switzerland more than a third of 16 year-olds are in part-time schooling. The participation rates of the 17 year-olds fall by 10 points or more in four of the seven countries considered (Japan is not included due to lack of data on enrolments in higher education by age). Still around or above 75 per cent of this age group remain in formal education with a growing proportion of part-time students in Germany and, above all, in Switzerland. Far wider

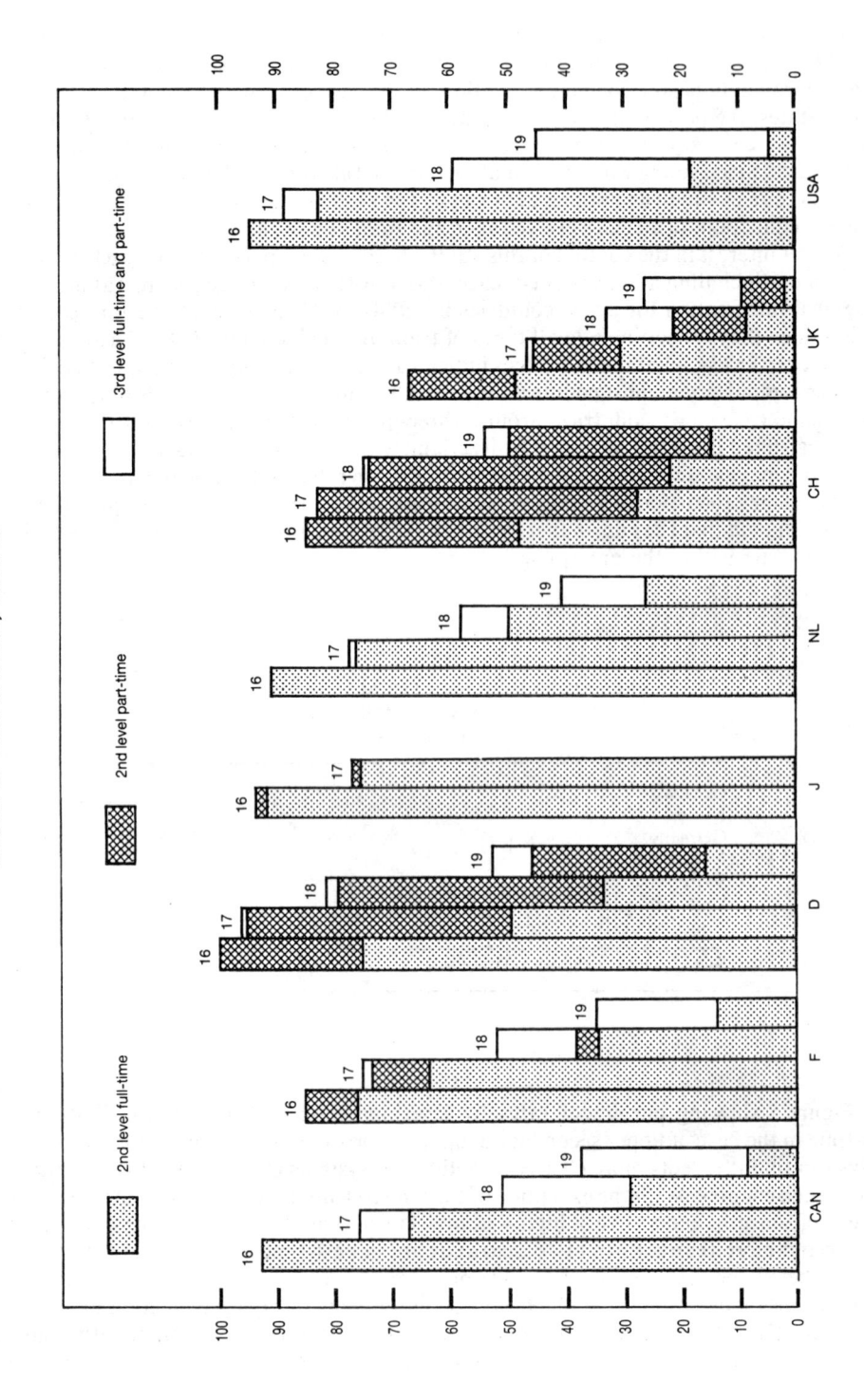

Figure 5. ENROLMENT RATES BY SINGLE YEAR OF AGE AND LEVEL OF EDUCATION, 1984/85

Source: OECD Educational Data Bank.

variations among countries are observed in the case of 18 year-olds where the structural differences between the educational systems seem to play a key role. The first factor is the even stronger dominance of part-time studies in countries like Switzerland and Germany where the dual system enrols more than 75 per cent of the 18 year-old student body. The second variable relates to the differences in the modal age at which young people complete their secondary school, and as a consequence are confronted with the alternative of continuing on to higher education or leaving the formal system. In countries where this break is at a relatively early age, as in the United States, the overall participation rates of the 18 year-olds witness a far sharper decline than in those where it takes place at a later stage, as is the case of Germany and Switzerland. The following figures on which Figure 5 has been based may serve to highlight this point.

ENROLMENT RATES
(all levels)
of 17, 18 and 19 year-olds
in Germany, Switzerland and the United States
1984/85

	17 years	18 years	19 years
Germany	96.1	81.5	52.8
Switzerland	82.8	74.6	53.8
United States	88.0	58.7	44.5

Finally, the above table, taken together with Figure 5, reflects also the influence of different structural arrangements on the participation rates of 19 year-olds. In Germany and Switzerland more than half of this age group is still in formal education, the majority in the dual system (part-time schooling) and relatively few in higher education. The opposite situation is found in the other countries where, with the exception of the Netherlands, enrolment rates are far higher at the post-secondary level, nearly ten times so in the case of the United States.

Two further observations can be made on the basis of the preceding figures. First, it is clear that *one, and in some cases more than one, year of post-compulsory education is now the norm in most of the countries.* This modifies the conception of the "voluntary" nature of the participation, and indeed tends to blur the compulsory/post-compulsory demarcation. Secondly, the figures suggest that, contrary to what some advocates of recurrent education have expected, the recent trend has been towards the gradual extension of initial education, and an increasing "front-end-loading" of the system. An upturn in economic growth might suck some of these enrolments back into the youth labour market in some countries, particularly among the lower-level and more alienated groups, but it is also possible that governments which started new training schemes primarily to cope with youth unemployment will continue them for a different reason, namely to upgrade their workforce. Likewise, employers who have grown accustomed to having at least the first year of training subsidised may be loath to revert to a situation where they have to select and train from scratch again.

This chapter has attempted to paint a general picture of structures and trends in post-compulsory education in the eleven countries in terms of contextual factors, educational and training structures and current trends. More detailed information, including some on wastage or drop-out rates, is given in the case studies, where it can be related more meaningfully to the structures and policies in each country. Having established a broad conceptual and descriptive framework, the report will now turn to the analysis of the case studies themselves.

IV

THE TRIPARTITE DIVISION

1. The relationship between the three tracks

The first, broad set of questions which the authors of the case studies were asked to address related to the existence of the three main tracks or types of post-compulsory education, and the relationship between them. The questions were as follows:
- To what extent can the current system be classified in terms of general, technical and vocational streams? To what extent are these categories merging or changing? Are new forms of differentiation emerging? What are the main factors accounting for changing patterns of differentiation?
- Has there been any significant shift of emphasis on the three in recent years, in terms of numbers, resources or the composition of the student body (i.e. age, social origin, gender)? To what are these changes due: student preferences and demand? Government policy? Employer influence?
- To what extent do current policies encourage the integration or separation of different streams? Do they encourage progression from lower to higher streams? Do they facilitate transfer between different streams?

The questions thus addressed one of the basic issues of the study. Did the tripartite classification still hold? If so, why? If not, why not?

The conceptual analysis in Chapter II implied that the tripartite typology was not simply one of "content" but involved three dimensions: educational stage, cognitive level and employment sector. What also became clear from the studies was that the typology reflects two kinds of variables, those to do with the labour market, and those to do with the educational system, and the interaction between them.

A number of recent OECD reports have explored the implications for education and training of changes in work patterns in both the secondary and tertiary employment sectors[4]. There is no room in this report to describe their conclusions in any detail, but they complement this study very usefully. In general, they point to a greater fluidity in the organisation and content of work in many occupations. While the traditional vertical distinctions (e.g. between operative, supervisor, line manager) and horizontal demarcations (e.g. between tasks, jobs and occupations) have not suddenly disappeared, they are becoming less clear-cut, not only in the newer service occupations but also in some forms of traditional manufacturing. Such distinctions are social as well as occupational, and their permanence or transience reflect cultural factors which differ from one society to another. But in general the world of employment is less stable not only technologically but organisationally than it used to be and work, learning and innovation are becoming increasingly intertwined[7].

While the authors of the case studies were asked to concentrate on the education system rather than the labour market, changes such as those described above were frequently referred to, most explicitly in the Swedish study:

> "Technical and organisational changes at work have made a great difference to the organisation and content of vocational education in the 1970s and 1980s. The modular principle can be seen as a reflection of new production concepts in industry. In contrast to the far-reaching job fragmentation and specialisation of the 1960s, the automated production of the 1980s is accompanied by broad-based skills. The vocational lines of the upper secondary school are too rigid and narrow to fit in with the demands of the 1980s for diversity and preparedness for change in the skills context. This is not only true of industrial employment. Skills requirements in nursing and care are undergoing similar changes. The skills requirements of the 1980s also mean less emphasis on manual skills and more on systematic understanding and capacity for learning. The demands made on the skilled worker are approaching those traditionally made on production engineers. Similarly, caring skills are evolving towards greater emphasis on theoretical schooling and understanding." (Country study: Sweden, page 20).

While such arguments may apply with varying force to various occupations and levels of work within them, they point towards a post-compulsory system which, while continuing to be differentiated in terms of occupations and levels, is more fluid than past systems both in terms of vertical progression and lateral movement.

However, the typology of post-compulsory curricula reflects not only the labour market but the education system itself. Post-compulsory education builds on the final years of compulsory education, and changes at that stage obviously affect its structure and content. However, the case studies suggest that it is above all changes in higher and continuing education which have affected the post-compulsory stage in recent years, with the growth and diversification of access to higher education, and the widespread development of both formal and non-formal continuing education.

Whereas the traditional structure of the labour market tends to result in a *tripartite* sub-division at the post-compulsory stage, reflecting occupational and social stratification, the education system tends to impose a *binary* sub-division between those streams which normally lead on to higher education, and those which do not. The structure of post-compulsory education in any one country thus combines these two kinds of division, each of which is changing. This creates a complex and shifting pattern, with particular ambiguities about the "middle" (technical) stream, which may fall either side of the binary division. The underlying tripartite structure was discernible in almost all the case studies, but was most overt in a number of European countries: it is in fact a constant of French society and the education system that it has produced to think of studies in three sectors of preparation: general, technical and vocational.

> "The upper secondary school comprises: the lyceum (classical, scientific, artistic); the technical institutes (for industry, commerce, etc.) and teachers' institutes: and the vocational institutes (for industry, commerce, etc.) craft institutes and pre-primary teachers' colleges. This sub-division can be reconciled with the proposed division into general, technical and vocational education, with some caveats about intermediate or 'grey' areas." (Country study: Italy, p. 4.)

In the Netherlands, after at least 4 years in the first stage of secondary education pupils effectively have three options from which to choose.

"Even in the last three years of compulsory schooling, one finds mostly and in most cantons the three principal lines of study which feed the three main sectors of education and training for 15/16 to 18/19 year-olds. In precise terms, one finds:
- the line which makes the most theoretical and abstract demands which essentially feeds into long 2nd cycle general education and, partly, short general education, or high-level professional education;
- the line which makes moderate theoretical demands which feeds above all into short 2nd cycle education and the vocational sector (full-time or apprenticeship);
- the line which makes elementary theoretical demands which feeds almost exclusively into the sector of practical apprenticeships or basic vocational training." (Country study: Switzerland, p. 3.)

However, these and other case studies go on to describe a variety of ways in which the basic tripartite structure is being modified and loosened: alternative routes, bridging courses and opportunities for progression; attempts to upgrade the status of the lower level vocational courses (for example by giving them the prestigious title of *Baccalauréat* in France and *Maturità* in Italy); and the introduction of some common content in all courses, as in Sweden. Some of these changes seem to reflect labour market pressures to 'de-regulate' the system and make it more flexible; others seem to stem from the social pressures for greater equality of opportunity which infuenced policies in many countries in the 1970s and still have some force today. Despite all these changes, however, the underlying tripartite division seems to persist in many cases, even in a country as strongly committed to egalitarian policies as Sweden:

"In summary, general studies, technical studies and vocational studies are still quite separate entities in upper secondary school. The structure remains, but with somewhat altered status relationships, and a closer affinity between the subsystems as regards the subject content of their study programmes." (Country study: Sweden, p. 14.)

Even in the above countries, the binary division between those streams or lines which give access to higher education and those that do not is always present. However, it seems to be more marked in some of the case study countries than others. For example, both the United Kingdom case studies point to the relative isolation of "general" streams from technical and vocational ones.

"The prime aim of the general A-level stream is still regarded as gaining entry to degree courses, or equivalent. The degree for English and Welsh universities is normally three years, one of the shortest in Europe, and the A-level curriculum remains essentially specialist in order to underpin this. Recent initiatives to introduce AS levels are the latest in a long succession of suggestions on how to broaden the traditional A-level system. AS levels may be more successful than the other initiatives, but it is too early to say at the time of writing. This tradition of specialism tends to isolate the general stream from the others." (Country study: England and Wales, pp. 17-18.)

A greater emphasis on giving students from technical streams access to higher education, partly in order to flatten out the demographic downturn and partly to counteract potential shortages of technical and scientific manpower, may in time reduce this isolation, but it seems clear that in England and Wales at least, the essential distinction is between general on the one hand, and technical/vocational on the other. The distinction between technical and vocational has never been as clear in the United Kingdom as in some continental European countries, reflecting a historically less well regulated pattern of apprenticeship and perhaps a more pragmatic approach to such distinctions both in education and in the workplace.

Despite the fact that the pattern of technical/vocational education in Scotland is now markedly different from that south of the border, the essential division there too is between general and technical/vocational, the former having been largely left out of the recent reforms. The Scottish study analyses the distinction between the three types along five dimensions: certification, curriculum, institution, expected progression and relation to employment, and concludes that while the distinction between the general type and the others has become a little less distinct (with some school students taking vocational modules in addition to general courses) the technical and vocational types are now indistinguishable.

In Germany too, the essential distinction seems to be a binary one between general streams on the one hand, and technical/vocational ones on the other. The reasons are partly historical:

"The 'general' and 'vocational' sections have developed in clear separation from each other. Due to the educational philosophy conceived by Wilhelm von Humboldt and implemented by his associate (and successor as reformer and administrator Johann Wilhelm von Süvern), the Gymnasium has been defined as an academic institution which should expressly refrain from imparting any form of 'vocational' education to its pupils. It will be shown later than it is the fundamental affiliation with this traditional philosophy which confronts the current Gymnasium with substantial problems, because its position within the education system is primarily and distinctly defined as university-bound." (Country study: Germany, p. 7.)

On the other hand, the distinction between "technical" and "vocational" is largely a matter of mode of study:

"...it does not make any sense to draw a demarcation line between 'technical' and 'vocational' components in the current education system in Germany as far as the age-group between 15(16) and 18(19) is concerned. This argument can be reinforced by the official arrangement applied in today's policy-making and administration which treats all 'vocational' institutions as part of one section. It is true that one must make a distinction between full-time vocational schools and the 'dual' system. This distinction, however, does not congrue with the parallelism of technical and vocational schools in other national systems, because the relationship between their internal qualification structures and the occupational hierarchy overlaps the co-existence of both 'vocational' school types." (Country study: Germany, pp. 7-8.)

It was noted earlier that the current pattern in Italy can be interpreted broadly in terms of the tripartite division into general, technical and vocational. However, proposals for the reform of the upper-secondary stage, which have been under discussion for some years, envisage some rapprochement of the general and technical streams:

"The basic aim of this reform is to go beyond the existing dichotomy between 'general' education and 'technical' education in order to succeed in creating a kind of secondary institution which would offer, within a single mould, different orientations based on differing professional foundations (between the ages of 15 and 17, according to the proposal). In simple terms, one could say that the future orientation of the upper secondary school would be a bit less 'general' and a bit less 'technical', but the issue is far from straightforward, because it is not only a matter of the level of professionalism, but also the means by which it is acquired". (Country study: Italy, p. 6.)

However, as the Italian study goes on to point out, it is not at all certain that such changes will be implemented, since the general package of reforms has been the subject of considerable disagreement and controversy. In fact, many changes are already taking place in a more experimental or pragmatic way: the introduction of skills into general education; the constant modernization of technical programmes; and reforms in the vocational courses organised both by the State (which tend to be rather general) and the regions (which tend to be more specific and technical). All in all, such changes point towards a mixing of the three streams, rather than a definite shift of emphasis towards one or the other. In Greece also, there are some examples of mixing and convergence between the otherwise distinct streams.

An interesting historical perspective on binary divisions at this stage of education is provided by the Yugoslav case study, which traces the evolution of upper secondary education in that country through four decades and four sets of reforms. One of the key aims of the more recent reforms has been the elimination of one of the main characteristics of the earlier systems: what is referred to as "dualism": "the difference between streams leading to university studies and those leading directly to employment". The 1974 reforms abolished a tripartite institutional structure, and put in place a comprehensive system of vocationally-directed education, involving two years of common studies, followed by two years of specialised studies, any stream of which could, in theory, lead either to employment or higher education. This 2+2 pattern has given way in the 1980s, in most parts of the country, to a 4-year specialist pattern, involving a major choice at the age of 14/15. The specialist lines are classified in terms of 8 levels and 21-25 fields of employment. While all of them notionally give access to higher education, there appear to be stronger links between some lines and university entry than others, although it seems unlikely that a distinct general line, leading exclusively to higher education, will re-emerge.

In some respects, the system in Quebec appears to be more like that in continental Europe than that in the rest of Canada or North America. As the study explains, the original tripartite structure "was designed to match the social stratification of occupations: craft to secondary, technical to college, and professional to university". The distribution of students among the three streams was based on the theoretical normal distribution of performance on intelligence tests. In fact, the current system comprises a tripartite structure (short vocational, long vocational, and general) at the lower secondary stage, of which the last two lines lead to a binary structure (professional, general) at the post compulsory (CEGEP) stage, the last of which gives access to higher education. The *Collèges d'enseignement général et professionnel* provide, as their name implies, a comprehensive range of general and professional courses for young people between the ages of 17 and 20 (not to mention an increasing number of adults), and comprise a distinct stage and unique route between lower secondary and higher education. The system in Quebec is now being changed, mainly to upgrade the short vocational streams, and encourage greater vertical progression generally. It should be noted that students can change programme during their studies at the CEGEP, and some 30 per cent do. This suggests a greater degree of flexibility within the system than its structure would imply, and also a certain attenuation of the binary divide. Indeed, the Quebec study speaks of the "warming-up" of the aspirations of those in the professional streams, in contrast to the more familiar "cooling-out" of those in general ones, an aspect or at least aspiration which is characteristic of all comprehensive systems at this stage.

The system of post-compulsory education for 16 to 19 year-olds in the United States is extremely diverse and flexible:

> "Institutions that provide education and training offer a wide range of entry and exit points, and most evidence a considerable capacity to adapt to change. Their operations,

as well as their financing, vary greatly from state to state, even within states. Some experts fault the system for its redundancy and lack of linkages among sectors, while others feel that such complexity contributes to its strength." (Country study: United States, p. iii.)

Two points in particular distinguish it from some of the systems described already. The first is the fact that the main choice-point for young people comes not at the formal end of compulsory education (usually 16) when the great majority (92 per cent in 1985) remain at school, but on the completion of high school at the age of 18, when approximately 56 per cent continue their studies in some form of post-secondary education – two-year or four-year colleges, or vocational-technical programmes of various kinds. A second distinguishing characteristic of post-compulsory education in the United States is the ubiquity of credit transfer arrangements which allow students to accumulate course credits across a range of courses, institutions, and on either a consecutive or intermittent basis. Such arrangements are increasingly being widened to cover various kinds of non-traditional institutions, non-formal education, and experiential learning.

While there are three main tracks of study within the U.S. high school, and in that sense it conforms to the basic tripartite pattern, each of those tracks gives not merely formal access, but real accessibility, to higher education:

"In 1980, 38.2 per cent of the high school students were in an academic track, 24.4 per cent were in a vocational-technical track, and 36.4 per cent were in a general education track. Students in different tracks usually have different plans for activities after high school. Those who expect to attend college are more likely to follow the academic track. However, the curriculum taken by students in high school does not seem to prevent them from going to college. A 1982 follow-up survey of the 1980 school seniors indicated that 37.8 per cent of the students who followed a vocational track in high school and 50.6 per cent of the general education track students had enrolled in post-secondary education (compared to 80.7 per cent of the academic track students)." (Country study: United States, p. 22.)

It is worth pointing out that the system of post-secondary education in the United States is large, and particularly in the community colleges, very flexible in terms of admissions requirements. Perhaps as a consequence the binary distinction between those streams which lead on to higher education, and those which do not, which is sharp in some countries, is much less clear-cut in the United States, and the progression of students from one stage or level to another is less predictably linear.

At first sight, the Japanese upper secondary school has a binary structure, with 72 per cent of students in the general stream, and 28 per cent in the vocational stream (1985 figures). However, both streams are subdivided into different curriculum types, which in the case of the general stream include more academic and less academic variants. An analysis of the destinations of school-leavers points to considerable differences within the general stream, of whom about 30 per cent enter higher education, 40 per cent take jobs and nearly 25 per cent go on to further vocational training. (Three-quarters of all students on vocational courses take jobs on graduation). The pattern is thus more complex, and less dissimilar from that in some of the other countries in this study, than might at first be thought.

The analysis so far suggests two main policy issues. First, if the labour market is moving away from traditional forms of *occupational* differentiation, is the tripartite *educational* structure that still exists in most of the countries becoming dysfunctional? Does post-compulsory education embody a type and degree of differentiation which is anachronistic? Is it now *over-regulated* by comparison with employment? At the very least, is there a time-lag between the structures and perceptions in the education system, and those that exist in the labour market? The Japanese study alludes to this:

"In view of the fact that large companies usually do offer better benefits, it is natural that people seek to enter those upper secondary schools whose graduates had excellent results in the entrance examinations of the most prestigious universities and those with the best records in placing their graduates in large private enterprises. The paradox here is that people have come to be influenced more by the hierarchical orders of schools in inverse proportion to the decreased value of university diplomas. In postwar Japanese society, which has witnessed great economic and political equalisation, the possession of university diplomas or even diplomas from elite universities does not necessarily ensure placement in a big company or of being promoted to its higher echelons. It is against this background that the elaborately differentiated system of upper secondary schools has developed." (Country study: Japan, p. 26.)

Secondly, the analysis has highlighted the importance of the educational division between courses which lead on to higher education and those which do not, a division stronger in some countries than others, but present to some degree in all the ones in this study. (This division is not only one of courses, but often of institutions and professional cadres as well). The educational reasons for that binary division are fairly obvious: higher education constitutes the apex of the educational system, and as such exercises a powerful gravitational pull, structurally and normatively, on the rest. It is not for nothing that it is called "higher". But it may be that this duality between what does and does not lead on to higher education, so important to those in the system and many outside it including students and parents, is actually dysfunctional for the labour market, because it erects a major educational demarcation which no longer corresponds to anything in the structure of employment. Increasingly, the labour market seems to be characterised by relative gradations rather than absolute distinctions, and if the education system were to mirror this, it would have to develop a more "graduated" and less rigid structure of courses and qualifications at both the post-compulsory and post-secondary levels.

The paradox is that while higher education in many countries has in fact developed in just such ways, particularly with the creation of non-university institutions[8], the streams that lead to it have often remained conservative in form (though not necessarily in content). As the following chapter will show, they and the qualifications to which they traditionally lead appear to have changed less than any other aspect of post-compulsory education. This suggests that it is the structure of *qualifications*, rather than the content of courses or pattern of institutions, which is the key modality of education at this stage, a point which will be explored further in the report. In this respect, the existence of a widespread system of credit transfer in the United States, and the developments in that direction in some other countries, such as Scotland and the Netherlands, are of particular interest, and it is worth emphasizing the distinction between formal access and real accessibility, which is demonstrated only by substantial flows of students into higher education from the relevant stream, and their relative success when they get there.

The second question about the general relationship between the three types or streams had to do with the balance between them. Had there been any significant shift of emphasis on the three in recent years, in terms of numbers, resources or the composition of the student body? If so, was the change due to government policy, market demand, or anything else? The reponses to this question are difficult to collate, because one cannot generate comparative data from non-comparable structures. However, some general observations can be made.

The implicit hypothesis here was that there would be a general shift in both numbers and policy emphasis from lower-level to higher-level types of courses, i.e. from vocational to technical, and technical to general. This would be consistent both with the displacement hypothesis and the need to upgrade the economy and workforce generally. It would also reflect the general "inflation" in educational and professional qualifications which has occurred in all countries, whereby better and better qualifications are needed for entry to the same job[9]. Such was the hypothesis; the reality is more complex, and reflects the employment value rather than educational status of the different streams.

There has been a general, upward shift in some countries, particularly if one takes the long view. For example, in Germany, between 1960 and 1985, the percentage of total enrolments increased for both the general streams (9 to 19 per cent) and full-time technical streams (12 to 21 per cent) but decreased for vocational (dual) streams, from 79 to 61 per cent. In France too, general and technical streams have increased substantially in the last decade. In Japan, between 1955 and 1985, the percentage in general upper secondary streams rose from 60 to 72 per cent, with a corresponding decline in vocational ones (there is now also a very small but growing technical sector which in Japan is given post-secondary status). By contrast, the percentage of students enrolled in the academic track in the United States fell from 46 in 1972 to 38 per cent in 1980, with a corresponding increase in the less demanding general track. In Italy, general streams showed a slight decline of about 1 per cent between 1976 and 1986, and technical and vocational streams a small increase (1.4 and 3.1 per cent). In Sweden, general streams declined substantially between 1970 and 1985 while enrolments in technical and vocational ones increased markedly. The proportions in Switzerland have remained relatively stable.

More detailed data on each country are given in the various case studies. While the figures cited here do not appear to support the "upgrading" hypothesis unequivocally in terms of *general* streams, the studies do point to the disappearance of *vocational* streams at the *lower secondary level*. Historically, such streams provided for those students who would leave education earliest and enter the labour market soonest. Now, the general increase in and prolongation of initial education means that such early leavers are at a general disadvantage in the labour market, and the specific and often practical skills they could offer are orientated towards precisely those kinds of employment which have suffered most in the recent economic recession. This situation seems to have affected the status of the relevant vocational courses in several countries; for example, the LBO courses in the Netherlands, the CAP in France and short vocational courses in Quebec. We are witnessing a general tendency to delay vocational education and training to the post-compulsory stage, although this does not preclude a pre-vocational element in compulsory education.

However, any overall shift towards general streams seems to have been modified or checked in some countries by increased *graduate* unemployment, government restrictions on access to higher education, or both. For example, in Italy, where the general streams have declined slightly in the last decade, this may reflect fears among some students that there would be little benefit to them in the end from proceeding to higher education. Concurrently, there has been a slight growth in technical and vocational streams. In Sweden too, where the balance has shifted against general streams, as the case study makes clear, this is linked to internal subject differentiation within higher education, which is in many countries linked to differential graduate unemployment rates:

"General study programmes in upper secondary school comprise the three year natural science, social science and liberal arts lines and the two-year social and artistic and practical lines, together with the music line, which is also of two years' duration. Between them these lines represent a quarter of first-time upper secondary school students, which is a good deal less than in the 1960s. The heavy expansion of vocational and technical studies has been matched by a steep decline in the popularity of general studies. It is above all the three-year economics line which has come to figure as an alternative to the three-year liberal arts and social science lines, while the four-year technology line has become an alternative to the three-year natural science line. This pattern of choice forms part of a long-term shift which has been in progress since the beginnings of the present century from humanities to technical and scientific skills as the foremost concern of general upper secondary schooling. Thus the aspirations of the Upper Secondary Schools Commission to give all upper secondary school study programmes a vocational reference have been realised through changed pupil preferences rather than through reforms of organisation and content." (Country study: Sweden, p. 22.)

It is worth emphasizing that students at this stage, rather than simply choosing or being allocated to a particular sector or course, can sometimes use the system to exercise their educational and employment preferences. As the Scottish case study points out, "snapshot" statistics do not show how students move through the system, sometimes crossing the main demarcations of our typology. In Germany, for example, an increasing number of students take a degree and then do an apprenticeship, or *vice versa*.

Government policies may also modify any generalised shift of emphasis from lower-level courses to higher-level ones. In the United Kingdom, for example, the major change which has occurred in the last decade has been the sharp decline in traditional apprenticeships, and the rapid growth of the Youth Training Scheme, originally one and now two years long. This now provides for some young people who would previously have done an apprenticeship; indeed in some fields, such as construction, electrical trades and hairdressing, the change has been more one of format than content. However, the YTS also provides initial training for large numbers of young people who in previous decades would have gone straight into work from school, usually in unskilled or semi-skilled jobs. Thus the YTS can be perceived both as a short-term response to youth unemployment, and a longer term response to the need to upgrade the workforce; a duality of perception which may change with time.

It is worth noting finally that some case studies, in answer to this question, stressed the need not to shift the emphasis between streams, but to improve each one in its own way. This point was made about France and in the Swiss study, and may reflect a relative stability in the emphasis on the three main sectors of post-compulsory education in those countries. But the search for better quality was a theme which surfaced in a number of the studies. Perhaps it signals a transition from a period where the main policy concern was with quantitative changes in this stage of education, to one when the emphasis will be more on qualitative ones: content, teaching, processes, retention rates, achievement, and outputs.

The third question concerned the relationships between the three main streams, and the issues to do with integration and separation, progression or "blind alleys", lateral and vertical transfer between lines, streams or sectors. These issues have already been touched on in the analysis of the other two questions. There is a general trend in most countries towards a "looser" tripartite structure where such a structure exists, a trend which reflects various factors: a social concern with access and equality; a need to rationalise and simplify the system for demographic or economic reasons; a growing tendency to look at this stage of education "as a whole"; and an attempt to overcome educational rigidities in relation to the labour market.

Over and above these general trends, there is a particular emphasis on making the system more flexible in several countries. Modularity is seen to be a key element in doing this in both the Netherlands, where more is planned, and Scotland, where it is now the standard format for two of the three main types of course (technical and vocational: indeed the modular Action Plan has helped to erode the technical/vocational distinction). In Japan, current debate is much concerned with the need for greater diversity and individuality in what has been recently criticised there as a rather rigid and competitive though in many ways very effective system. This had led to proposals for the reform both of curricula and examinations. The rationalisation and simplification of qualifications, particularly the plethora of vocational qualifications, is a current policy concern in the United Kingdom. In Sweden, the emphasis on flexibility is directed more at the structure of courses, and the advantages and disadvantages of having relatively distinct and self-contained lines of study.

The responses to the three initial case study questions can now be summarised as follows:

- The divisions between the three streams are still evident in many countries, but they are becoming less clear-cut and more fluid. In particular, it is becoming increasingly difficult to distinguish between technical and vocational streams, and differentiation is increasingly opening up within each stream. The main reasons for these changes are increased fluidity of the labour market and flexibility of access to higher education.
- There is no consistent shift of emphasis among the three streams. The key factor seems to be student demand based on employment prospects rather than government policy. Where general streams continue to offer good employment prospects, they have continued to grow; where they do not, one finds differential emphasis within such streams, or the relative growth of technical streams, or certain forms of vocational education. The main burden of coping with youth unemployment and disadvantage has fallen on vocational streams, which have become diversified as a result.
- Current policies seem to encourage flexibility rather than integration. They encourage progression and mobility between courses and streams rather than a common base or framework for all students. The situation varies from country to country, but the general trend seems to be towards differentiated but open systems, rather than comprehensive ones based on core or common curricula.

These issues will be explored in more detail in the following sections of the report.

2. General education

Of the three main types of post-compulsory education analysed in the case studies, "general" courses seem to have changed least. Reference has already been made to the relative stability and indeed isolation of "A levels" in England and Wales. A similar point is made about the somewhat different Scottish system:

> "... compared to the rapid and radical changes elsewhere at the post-compulsory level the general sector is resistant to change. There are symbolic as well as sectional interests attached to the present structure, and especially to the Higher grade examination, 'traditionally the holy of holies of Scottish education'." (Country study: Scotland, p. 24.)

This view of the traditional upper secondary general qualification and the courses that lead to it is mirrored in some continental European countries. The Italian case study speaks of the fear of "contamination" of traditional general education, and in France the orientation towards general education remains a constant in the education system. Some 75 per cent of parents and pupils want to have access to the long-cycle upper secondary courses, and even if one notes the remarkable increase in long-cycle technical enrolments in the last decade, these are still well below the level of those in general education. The role of the *baccalauréat général* in French society partly explains this constancy. Any attempt to alter access to it, or the content of it, meets with suspicion and an anxiety that is sometimes expressed with some vehemence.

In Germany and in the Netherlands also, though less so in Switzerland, there appears to be a relative stability about the general stream or sector which contrasts with the more substantial changes which are occurring in technical and vocational education, and the radical initiatives which are being taken to meet the needs of the "risk groups" in each country. Other studies refer to the status and importance of this stream, and its privileged connection with higher education. The Yugoslav study discusses the possible re-emergence of traditional general streams, despite a policy firmly committed to comprehensive principles. In Sweden, the connection between such streams and higher education has become stronger in the 1980s, reversing the trend towards more pluralistic access to higher education. The Quebec study notes the "gradual drift of college teaching towards university waters". And the Japanese study refers to the process whereby general streams regained their traditional elite status after a brief attempt at comprehensive reform immediately after World War II.

Why is general education at this level relatively stable? One answer must be historical; the qualifications to which it leads are often relatively old, by educational standards, and therefore well established. In the past, when much smaller proportions of the age group attained them, their status was even higher, and that historical glow continues to bathe today's much larger cohorts. In some countries too, in continental Europe, achievement of the relevant qualification (*baccalauréat, Abitur, matura, maturità*) gives constitutional rights of access to higher education which governments tamper with at their peril.

However, the situation revealed by the case studies is both more complex and more interesting than this. The statistics from some of the countries show a long-term trend towards increased enrolments in general courses. Whereas in the past, these catered for the often small minority of students who aspired to enter higher education, in the last decade they have grown to encompass 20 per cent, 30 per cent and even more of the age group. One could hypothesize, on the basis of this quantitative trend, that such expansion would lead to greater differentiation within general streams, simply because they are larger. And to the extent that either access to, or demand for, higher education does not keep pace with this expansion, one might expect to see an emerging distinction between higher-education orientated variants and more employment-orientated variants of general education. Moreover, such a distinction might not only affect the content of courses, but their ethos and style; not only the overt curriculum, but the "hidden curriculum". These hypotheses were implicit in the three questions about general streams:

- Have there been or are there any major plans for changes in general upper secondary streams, or their related qualifications?
- Are there any attempts to make general streams more employment-oriented? If so, how?
- To what extent is there a conflict of purpose or ethos between preparing students for higher education, and preparing them for employment?

The first thing that became apparent from the case studies was that despite the appearance of stability in general education at this stage, there was a good deal of movement, or attempted movement, going on in the detail of courses. Some of this seems to reflect a concern to update and modernise curricula, for example by incorporating some element of information technology. Other reforms, or proposed reforms, reflected problems or issues which seemed to be of particular national importance: the emphasis on academic standards and quality in the United States; on greater flexibility in both content and teaching in Japan; on technological studies and greater breadth in the United Kingdom; on the balance of requirements and options in both the Netherlands and Germany; and on the balance between "classical" and "modern", disciplinary and interdisciplinary studies in the latter; on the right mix of "normal" and "intensive" courses in Switzerland; and on "process" rather than "content" in a number of countries.

As regards the general questions put to the authors, the responses fall into two broad categories. In a few countries, the expansion of general education has led to a formal division between two streams, usually short-cycle and long-cycle general education. However, in the majority of the case-study countries, expansion has led to change, either planned or unplanned, within the single general education streams. The clearest examples of the former – the emergence of "dual" streams – are in Switzerland, the Netherlands and the United Kingdom.

In Switzerland, there are in fact three distinct forms of "general" education: 3.5/4-year long-cycle courses leading to 5 different types of *maturité* (= *baccalauréat*), which enrol 12.6 per cent of the age-group; 2 to 3-year short-cycle streams leading to a general diploma, enrolling 2.7 per cent of the age group; and a one-year general, transitional, pre-vocational course which enrols 9 per cent of the age group. However, the term general education is typically applied only to the first two, which together enrol 15.3 per cent of the age group. This is not a high percentage relative to the other countries in the study, so why has it been necessary to sub-divide general education at all? The answer seems to be that the current sub-divisions at the post-compulsory stage correspond well to both the interests of students and the needs of the Swiss labour market. The short-cycle general line suits students "who do not want to follow studies which are too remote from their centre of interest". The structure of the line combines a general foundation (*tronc*) which covers languages, mathematics, natural and social sciences, and artistic and physical education, with one of three pre-vocational options: para-medical, socio-educational, or administrative. Certain changes are being introduced into these short-cycle general courses (notably an extension from 2 to 3 years) but the evidence suggests that they are both attracting a growing number of students and finding a niche in the labour market, especially the service sector.

In the Netherlands, there is an institutional distinction between pre-university courses and general courses which may lead on to other forms of higher education, notably higher vocational education and teacher education. As the diagram of the Dutch system shows (see Figure 6), the secondary grammar schools (VWO) typically lead on to university, whereas the senior general secondary schools (HAVO) lead on to other forms of higher education. (The system allows for progression from HAVO to VWO as well; and likewise from junior general (MAVO to HAVO). Thus the sub-division of general education at the upper secondary level in the Netherlands reflects a dual system of *higher education* which has been well established for some decades. Since higher education is the main point of reference for general streams at this level, such a sub-division is therefore logical, and the balance of emphasis on the two sub-types is likely to reflect the balance of emphasis on the two forms of higher education. It is worth noting, in passing, that major reforms are in fact underway in the Dutch university system.

The fact that, despite the long-term increase in the enrolments in general streams, only two out of the eleven countries have developed distinct non-academic variants of these streams suggests a problem, and one that was identified in the Scottish study. The belief that the expansion of general education necessitates the development of pre-academic and pre-employment variants is based on the assumption that employers recruit on the basis of relevant knowledge and skills. However, this is not always the case.

Figure 6. **DIAGRAM OF THE DUTCH EDUCATION SYSTEM**

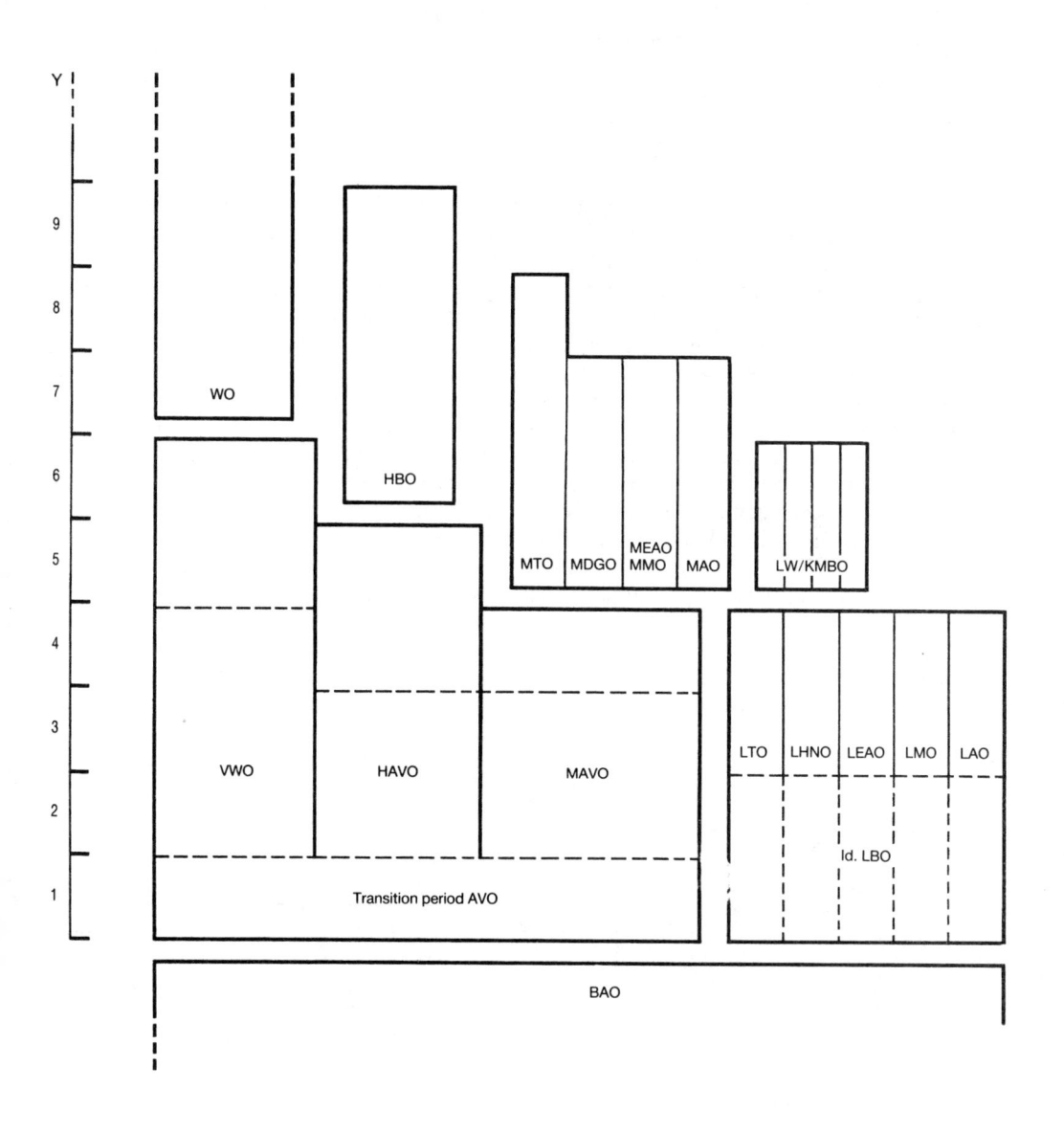

BAO	=	basisonderwijs = primary education
LBO	=	lager beroepsonderwijs = junior vocational (pre-vocational) education
MAVO	=	middelbaar algemeen voortgezet onderwijs = junior secondary education
HAVO	=	hoger algemeen voortgezet onderwijs = senior general secondary education
VWO	=	voorbereidend wetenschappelijk onderwijs = pre-university education
LW, KMBO	=	apprenticeships; full-time vocational education
MBO	=	middelbaar beroepsonderwijs = technical education
HBO	=	hoger beroepsonderwijs = higher professional education
WO	=	wetenschappelijk onderwijs = university education

"Employers' recruitment and selection criteria tend to reinforce established academic hierarchies with respect to pre-employment and especially school courses. In other words employers tend to prefer young people with the qualifications and subjects that carry highest academic status, largely on the grounds that they are seeking general potential rather than specific skills or knowledge and that the 'best' students will have entered and succeeded in the high-status academic courses. Thus, when employers recruit students from school courses their selection criteria may not conflict with those of higher education." (Country study: Scotland, p. 27.)

The dilemma facing non-academic general courses can be analysed in terms of Figure 7 below. Employers may recruit either on the basis of ready-to-use knowledge and skills (competence, or at a higher level, expertise) or on the basis of inferred general ability, or both. The emphasis varies from one occupation and one level of work to another. The highest status courses should therefore be those which guarantee both high levels of expertise/competence, and high levels of general ability, as measured indirectly by norm-referenced access and achievement. At the upper secondary stage, no streams or subjects meet both these criteria (A), since those students of high ability have not yet developed high competence (as many will by the end of their first degree, for example) and those students who have developed high competence (e.g. in craft skills) are usually drawn from the lower (cognitive) ability quartiles. What general streams at this stage seem to offer is (B): the guarantee of high ability (and with it trainability in both cognitive and affective terms) at the expense of low competence. This is what higher education is looking for, and what many employers are looking for too, since they reckon that the training costs involved are more than compensated for by the potential returns on having an able employee. By contrast, specific vocational courses and apprenticeships offer

Figure 7. **ABILITY AND COMPETENCE**

	Ability High	**Ability** Low
Competence High	A	C
Competence Low	B	D

ready competence or skills (C), without any pretensions to high-level general ability, and these again have their place and value in the labour market.

The problem for non-academic general courses is that they risk slipping from (B) to (D), which guarantees neither ability nor competence. Indeed, one can now understand why the term "general" can refer to the highest streams in some cases and lower ones in others. It would seem that non-academic general courses are only likely to succeed if they manage to guarantee moderate levels of both ability and competence, through a relatively rigorous general education, and a reasonably thorough vocational preparation in certain, well-targeted occupations. That description appears to fit the Swiss short cycle general course, and may indeed account for its evident success. The new Certificate of Pre-Vocational Education in the United Kingdom also has this general+vocational course framework, but although it is described as an all-ability option, it appears at present to be recruiting mainly from among the moderately or less able students in the age group, and may therefore risk the kind of slippage described above.

If most countries have not formally divided general education into academic and employment variants, how have the enlarged general streams become differentiated? In most cases, through subjects. Several studies report a growing divergence, within general streams, between mathematics and science lines on the one hand, and humanities/social science lines on the other. This is the case in Sweden:

"The natural science line has set a standard for the qualifications required of post-secondary students. The character of this line as a royal road to higher education has been further accentuated in the 1980s by a series of measures favouring direct transition from upper secondary school to higher education, at the same time loading the dice against mature students and 'supplementary students'. Today, ten years after the higher education reform, the natural science line has consolidated its position as a university entrance programme, at the same time as the status of the social line has been further weakened in terms of both credential value for admission to attractive post-secondary programmes and popularity with students." (Country study: Sweden, p. 23.)

The Quebec study was also concerned with this kind of internal differentiation within general education, and even within social science lines:

"The science line is tending to become the royal road to access to university studies, whatever the subsequent direction chosen. By contrast, the social science line without mathematics is tending to become the dead end for those who do not know where to go, and the completion rates in it are very low." (Country study: Quebec, Canada, p. 32.)

The difference between the natural and social science lines in the CEGEPs also results in different course structures, largely prescribed and centripetal in the sciences, but much more optional and centrifugal in the social sciences.

While the contrasts between science and social science programmes may not be quite so strong in other countries, there is often nevertheless a pecking order among different lines of study or subjects which is related to the relative difficulty of admission to different faculties or departments in higher education institutions. This is the case with the different types of French *baccalauréat*, with the prestigious *Bac C* keeping all options open. In countries where medical or natural science faculties have restricted access (through a formal or *de facto numerus clausus*) and arts and social sciences ones are relatively open, the difference in status has become more marked in recent years, through growing disparities in staff student ratios and units of resource. Such trends have meant that the arts and social sciences have become associated not only with easy access, but poor conditions, high drop-out and graduate unemployment. The implicit two-class structure of higher education reproduces itself at the post-compulsory stage in the internal differentiation of the general stream and its related qualifications.

If large general education streams tend to be differentiated, then Japan which has the largest, should also have the most differentiated. In Japan, 93 per cent of the age group are enrolled in upper secondary schools, and of these, 72 per cent were following "academic/general" courses in 1985. Thus for the great majority of Japanese young people, post-compulsory education means general education, a fact which contrasts with the situation in European countries, where the proportion is likely to be less than a third or even a quarter, and in Japan the trend has been towards general education and away from vocational/special education for the last ten years. In fact, the Japanese system is more differentiated than these aggregate figures might suggest. To begin with, many general subjects have a practical variant (A) and an academic variant (B). These are combined in various ways in four major curriculum categories, with the emphasis respectively on (I) humanities, (II) science, (III) humanities and science and (IV) vocational/specialised. While the first three give access to higher education, the fourth tends to lead on to employment and further vocational training in a special training school. In 1985, whereas 39 per cent of upper secondary graduates entered higher education, and 25 per cent took jobs, 30 per cent went on to further training. Thus the general education stream in Japan shows a considerable degree of internal differentiation both in terms of curriculum and subsequent activity, not to mention institutional status. Current policies seem to be aimed at more variety, both in the curriculum (some reduction in core requirements and increase in options) and teaching (use of a wider range of methods) as the system attempts to cope with an intake that is increasingly diverse in terms of abilities, attitudes and motivation.

Why does such differentiation take the form that it does? Why, in particular, do mathematics and the natural sciences seem to come out top in the pecking-order of subjects in so many countries? Historical factors may give a particular status to classical studies in some countries, such as Italy; and English language has a status equal to mathematics and natural science in Japan. The answer seems to involve a mixture of cultural and educational factors. Culturally, science and technology are central to late twentieth century society. They provide much of the basis of our way of life. They are still linked, despite misgivings, to the idea of progress. They form the core expertise of many high-level jobs and research. However, the educational status of such subjects seems to rest on something different: the fact that, in the eyes of many educators, employers and of the general public, they are *demanding*, and thus a good test of cognitive ability. Their reputation for difficulty seems to rest on several things. First, they involve specialised, hieratic codes which are quite different from natural language. Secondly, they appear to be quite remote from ordinary experience and common sense knowledge, and to test logic and abstract reasoning. Thirdly, they seem to demand a long, linear initiation. One can see how, in these terms, the arts and social sciences, which are couched more in natural language and draw on common perceptions and experience, and are accessible at many points and in many ways, may be thought (however mistakenly) to be less cognitively demanding and thus a poorer indicator of general intellectual ability. It is worth remembering, too, that in the past, some of the most prestigious subjects (such as classical languages) shared some of these characteristics of "difficulty".

However simplistic such ideas seem, especially to those in the humanities and social sciences, the fact remains that these perceptions of relative difficulty seem to be widespread. One measure of them is the lack of reciprocity in transfers between science and non-science lines of study: science to non-science is easy, non-science to science is difficult. However, what is probably more important is the different value of different subjects as measures of inferred general ability (see Figure 7). In this respect, mathematics and the natural sciences have an indirect, and even symbolic, importance in current systems as indirect measures of ability which is distinct from their "real" relevance to higher education or employment.

What has emerged from this analysis of "general" streams at the post-secondary stage? The basic issue seems to be as follows. Historically, such streams came into being primarily to prepare students for university: in terms of Figure 1, they constituted the general or foundation stage of what can be regarded as a long-cycle academic or professional education which reaches its conclusion only with the completion of undergraduate or even post-graduate studies. As such they had a clear and unambiguous function. Of course there were still issues to be debated and resolved within those parameters. How broad should the foundation be? Should certain subjects be required of all students? Should the structure of studies be aligned with the structure of faculties and disciplines in higher education, or would an interdisciplinary approach provide a better foundation? Should completion of the stage give access to all faculties or should there be a more precise relationship between the subjects studied and faculty entered? Different countries answered these questions in different ways, and still do; but there was a fundamental consensus about the purpose of general education at the upper secondary level, a consensus embodied as much in the process and ethos of such courses as in their content: the special "feel" of the upper *lycée*, *licei*, *Gymnasium*, or sixth form, which anticipated and socialised students in preparation for the academic world.

Where both post-compulsory education and higher education have expanded in parallel, each appears to have become more differentiated. This is perhaps clearest in those countries with the largest proportions of the age group enrolled in each sector. But nearly all OECD countries expanded their higher education systems dramatically in the 1960s and 1970s, leading to the expansion of general streams at the post-compulsory stage. However, at risk of oversimplifying, one can now draw a contrast between, on the one hand, some European countries, in which general streams are criticised for remaining too tightly geared to higher education, and on the other hand, the United States, where they are currently criticised for not being geared tightly enough, and thus not providing an adequate academic foundation. This has led to the recommendation, in the report entitled *A Nation at Risk*[10], that all students seeking a high school diploma should be required to lay the foundations in the "five new basics": English, mathematics, science, social studies, computer science, and (for the college-bound) a foreign language. Such proposals raise the question of the curricular relationship between upper secondary general streams and higher education. Currently, students in such streams may study anything from two or three subjects at "Advanced level" in the United Kingdom to six or seven in some continental European countries. As noted above, the patterns and requirements vary greatly; can anything general be said?

In principle, the structure of pre-academic general streams is governed by three main considerations. First, they need to include subjects which provide not merely a foundation for the advanced study of the same subject in higher education, but which underpin a whole range of subjects. This suggests that such streams should include mathematics which is essential to the study of the sciences and to a lesser extent the social sciences, and a first and possibly second language to give an *entrée* into the humanities and social sciences in one or more cultures. (Language is sometimes seen merely as a matter of enabling students to express themselves and communicate clearly, but this is a narrow view. Just as there are various branches of mathematics, so there are various uses and registers of language, and linguistic competence is a prerequisite not merely of communication but of conceptualisation, abstract thought and cultural understanding.) Computing can also lay increasing claim to be added to this small list of subjects which "unlock" a range of other subjects, particularly in relation to technology.

Beyond these three or four key subjects, much depends on the curricular pattern in higher education itself. Where the student enters a particular faculty in higher education – science, social science, or humanities, for example – the pre-academic stream may need to offer some foundation studies for that faculty, in the form of two or three subjects or some kind of interdisciplinary course. Where however the first year or two of higher education is broader, and faculty or subject specialisation is delayed, as is the case in the United States, there are arguments for continuing pre-academic studies in all the main faculty areas – science, social science, humanities, etc.

However, all such patterns come up against the problem that by this relatively advanced stage of education many students display differential abilities for and interest in different subjects. Some find it extremely difficult if not impossible to cope with the study of mathematics, science, literature or a foreign language at an advanced level. This suggests that of the range of subjects studied, students should be allowed to take some at a higher level, and others at a less advanced level which nevertheless aims at a reasonable level of competence and ensures continuing contact with that subject.

In general terms, these considerations point towards a typical pre-academic stream consisting of around six subjects, half of which might be taken at a higher level, and half at a lower level. However, in practice, the main determinant of the pattern of the pre-academic stream in each country is the pattern of the higher education in that country. As long as these patterns remain as various as they are, there seems little likelihood that national pre-academic curricula will converge, despite initiatives such as the *International Baccalauréat*.

Where the expansion of upper secondary education and higher education have not matched each other, a more overt form of differentiation emerges: that between preparation for higher education and preparation for employment. This can come about either because upper secondary education produces an "oversupply" of applicants for entry to higher education, or because the demand for higher education from qualified applicants falls, in response to graduate unemployment. In either case, the relationship between general streams and higher education becomes less clear-cut.

This means that the previously single-minded general stream has to become dual purpose, creating problems which were identified in both the French and German systems, among others.

In France, given the character of the *baccalauréat général* and its almost exclusive objective of preparation for entry to higher education, any orientation of the general streams towards preparation for employment seems largely excluded. In fact, the objective of a fundamental general education which preparation for higher education implies is difficult to reconcile with the specific objectives required by preparation for employment. Besides, it would be very difficult to maintain, side by side, general streams which prepared students for employment (which could only be tertiary employment) and the vocational streams which already exist, or even the technical streams which, for some, provide a preparation for professional life, either immediately after the technical *baccalauréat*, or after further training in courses for high-level technicians or at the IUT (*Institut universitaire de technologie*).

A similar tension is described in the German system:

"It is true that the upper stage, even in its reformed shape, has definitely resumed the traditional concept of the German *Gymnasium* which defines this school type as purely pre-academic and preparatory with regard to university requirements. On the other hand it has been increasingly exposed to the immediate expectations and requirements of the employment system which are caused by changing attitudes among youngsters and their parents who have begun to regard it as having an alternative function as a 'prevocational' institution, though within the general education section. Therefore one can conclude that below the official maintenance of the traditional philosophy the 'reformed upper stage' of the *Gymnasium* is about to be reshaped into an institution which in fact becomes more and more considered as an avenue to (advanced) vocational training or even to direct transition into a job or work besides continuing its pre-academic function. Recent developments even signal an increasing orientation of *Gymnasium* leaving certificate holders to training schemes in the 'dual' (apprenticeship) system. They constituted 25 per cent of certificate holders in 1985, whereas in 1971 approximately 90 per cent aspired to enter university directly." (Country study: Germany, p. 9.)

Thus the straightforward historical link between general upper secondary streams and higher education is no longer straightforward. Another complicating trend is already evident in some countries: the diversification of higher education intake to include "non-traditional" students of various kinds. Non-traditional in this context usually means adult students, "unqualified" students or both; the definition is loose, but the essential point is that such students do not enter higher education from the normal secondary school streams. Such policies have been advocated for some years, particularly under the rubric of "recurrent education", but what policy failed to achieve in some countries, demographic necessity is now bringing about. This trend is even affecting the post-compulsory sector in some countries, with increased adult enrolments in the CEGEPs in Quebec and Further Education Colleges in the United Kingdom. As mentioned earlier, this signals a shift of emphasis from "tertiary" to "community" institutions in some countries, and indeed the community colleges in the United States are perhaps the prime example of institutions which cater for both school leavers and older adults. Such a trend also points to a more intermittent pattern of attendance at the post-compulsory stage, which may have implications for the structure of courses and qualifications.

This report has concentrated on the problems posed for general streams by their changing relationship with higher education. It has analysed briefly the two main responses to the problem: sub-divide the general stream into two, or increase the differentiation within the single academic-type stream. It may be, however, that the solution to the problem lies not at this level at all, but in higher education. Since higher education is the main point of reference for general streams, it is logical to suppose that only changes in it can resolve problems at the post-compulsory stage. The fact that the binary distinction between streams which lead on to higher education and those which do not is still so strong in many systems suggests that higher education is itself an all-or-nothing matter in some countries. Compared to the complex gradations and movements of the employment market, it still often appears monolithic and unilinear.

In fact, many developments in recent years have made it much less so. The development of short-cycle institutions in various countries provides an alternative to the full-length traditional pattern. Entrance requirements have become more flexible. The spread of modular credit schemes has made transfer and alternation of studies easier. But somehow, in the European countries at least, the distinction between what is and is not higher education continues to permeate education systems, at the post-compulsory stage. By contrast, the system which has developed over a long period of time in the United States appears more flexible. There, as the case study notes, few student decisions at the post-compulsory stage are irreversible. The reason for this seems to lie not so much in the pattern of institutions (some European countries have as wide an array) but in the structure of courses, entrance requirements and qualifications. In the U.S. system the course, not the subject, is the fundamental curriculum unit.

While it would be simplistic to merely contrast subject-based curricula with course-based ones, the difference is significant. Curricula which are conceived in terms of subjects tend to be conceptualised in terms of educational or academic logic, and ultimately in terms of the structure of disciplines and faculties which forms the traditional basis for higher education. By contrast, the concept of the "course" is open to multiple frames of reference: not only the academic frame, which continues to be important, but also considerations related to society, employment, individual needs and personal development. A course-based system is less likely to erect a sharp distinction between what is or is not higher education. As the German case study makes clear, this tension between subjects and courses as the fundamental curricular unit has underlain much of the debate about the *Gymnasium* in the last decade and more, with recent trends seeming to re-establish the more traditional subject-based approach.

The distinction between subjects and courses bears on the final question put to the authors of the case studies: To what extent is there a conflict of purpose or ethos between preparing students for higher education, and preparing them for employment? It is worth noting, first of all, that this question seemed to make more sense to the European authors than the non-European ones. The fact that large Japanese employers automatically recruit their high-level staff from the most prestigious universities, and the fact that over a quarter of all entrants to U.S. higher education in 1985 intended to major in business studies suggests that the question about ethos was perhaps unconsciously a Euro-centric one. In some European countries, higher education has historically had closer affinities with the *tertiary* employment sector, and in particular with the civil service and the professions, than with manufacturing industry. Indeed, it has been argued that higher education in some countries has contributed to an anti-industrial ethos[11].

The question of the "ethos" or "culture" of general education is best left to the chapter on content and process, where it can be treated as an aspect of the "hidden curriculum". Here, suffice to say that the whole drift of education policy in the 1980s has been to link education, employment and the economy more closely, and that this shift has shown itself not only in policy initiatives but in the pattern of student demand, which has veered generally towards employment relevance.

3. Technical education

Although the links between general streams and higher education are becoming more complex and less exclusive on both sides, higher education still provides such streams with a dominant point of reference. It suggests what they should be about. The situation of technical streams, however, has never been quite as clear, perhaps because their point of reference is not higher education but the labour market, a labour market in which roles, functions, occupations and skills are subject to continual and often unpredictable change. It may be useful, therefore, to begin this section with some general comments about the nature of technical education at the post-compulsory stage.

As the very term "technical" implies, this stream developed historically in relation to the secondary (manufacturing) sector. Although the Greek roots of the term (connoting arts and skills) are of course very old, the modern educational and economic use of the word dates from the industrial revolution. Before the industrial revolution, there was general education (typically of a scholastic or classical kind) and there was vocational education, especially that organised by the craft and commercial guilds in European countries. But "technical" implies the application of science to production, a development which did not become generalised until the nineteenth century, despite earlier more random attempts. This fact helps to explain one of the key characteristics, and problems, of technical courses: the relationship between theory and practice. In general education, there may be theory, but there is usually little concept of practice, since the relationship between what is studied and the work that people eventually do is indirect and elastic. Conversely, in vocational courses leading to semi-skilled or skilled jobs, there is little reference to theory, though perhaps more now than in the past, as operations come to depend more on cognition and less on manipulation. But it is in technical or technician-level courses that the characteristic relationship and tension between theory and practice is found. Indeed, if one comes across complaints from practitioners that courses are too abstract and remote from the real world, or from teachers that employers are short-sighted and narrow-minded, it is a sure sign that one has found a technical course.

Perhaps because there is a substantial theoretical element in such courses, they tend to be full-time rather than part-time; indeed the statistics given in Chapter III use this simple criterion rather than the problematic one of "level" in distinguishing between different types of technical/vocational education. Such full-time courses will of course include practical sessions in workshops or laboratories as well as classroom teaching, and may involve placements or field studies outside the institution. Nevertheless, the fact that they are full-time means that in terms of format at least, they are closer to general courses than part-time vocational training or apprenticeship.

The affinity is not only one of form: technical courses typically include some general education content as well, though the proportion of this varies from country to country. Where there is a long and well-established tradition of technical education, the general education element is often substantial. This allows such streams to claim that they are not "merely" technical i.e. that they cover wider issues and perspectives as well. It also facilitates progression to higher education, at least on paper.

One further point should be made. The term "technical" which has its origins in manufacturing, has over the years become broadened to cover all kinds of jobs that involve some application of theory to practice, whether it be in office administration, health care, commerce, agriculture, or other fields. In some cases, the label seems odd and unnatural, perhaps because the process of "application" of organised knowledge to practical problems is less clear-cut than it is in the manufacturing field. Indeed, there may be pressure on such fields to develop their own "theory", and a counter-reaction among practitioners against what is seen as a form of "academic drift". This tension is observable in traditional fields as different as nursing, commerce and catering, but it is also difficult to define the role or nature of the technical in new and well-less formed fields, such as information technology. The concept of technician, is, after all, both an epistemological and an occupational one, connoting not only a body of knowledge but a body of people.

Such comments suggest that there might be particular problems in both formulating and responding to questions about technical education at the post-compulsory stage, and this was indeed the case. The questions were as follows:

- To what extent is there a convergence between the concepts of general education and technical education?
- Is there a clear distinction between technical and vocational streams?
- Have changes in the structure of employment or in the nature of technology itself led to major changes in the organisation or content of technical courses?

The first thing to be said is that although the *concept* of technical education is familiar enough in all countries, distinct technical *streams* or *types* only exist in some. Such streams are clearly defined in France, Italy and Sweden, where they enrol substantial percentages of the age group. There are identifiable technical sectors in other continental European countries (Germany, the Netherlands, Switzerland) but the distinction there between technical and vocational is primarily one of the mode of study (full-time vs. "dual"). In the United Kingdom it is more difficult to identify a technical stream, though one can point to technician-level courses at both the post-compulsory and post-secondary stages. In Yugoslavia, all streams at this stage notionally have a labour-market outlet, but some streams lead typically to the middle levels (III, IV, V) of employment and hence could be regarded as technical. In Quebec, the *cours professionnels* in the CEGEPs are at a higher level than the compulsory vocational streams, but distinct from the pre-university general ones, and could therefore count as "technical". In the United States, most courses of this level or type occur at the post-secondary stage, in community colleges, proprietary colleges, or other forms of public and private training; it is not possible to identify a distinct and homogeneous technical sector. In Japan the great bulk of technical education takes place in higher education or on the job.

There is thus a good deal of structural diversity in technical education among the case study countries. However, there does seem to be some consensus that whereas technical courses are distinguished from general courses mainly by their *content*, they are distinguished from vocational courses mainly by their *level*. Thus the first two questions about the distinctions between technical streams and the other two required different kinds of answers, involving different criteria. This point has interesting implications for the convergence of streams. Any convergence between technical and general streams involves reconciling differences of content, which may be done by including a larger element of general studies in technical education, or by making general education more technologically-orientated. By contrast, any convergence of technical and vocational streams involves changes in cognitive or theoretical levels – either downgrading the demands made in technical education, or, more likely, upgrading vocational streams by making them more theoretically demanding. This perhaps helps to explain why the first kind of convergence has taken place in some systems (with technical education effectively being upgraded to the post-secondary stage) and the second (merging of the technical and vocational) in others. Indeed, one may find both within one system. In Sweden, whereas middle-level courses in the caring occupations have been upgraded to higher education, those in industrial occupations are still found primarily at the upper secondary stage, while commercial and administrative courses are found at both. As was pointed out in Chapter II, the analysis of streams involves not only "levels" but "sectors" and "stages", and the pattern may be differentiated along all three dimensions. And where new occupations and fields develop rapidly, as for example in information technology or some personal service fields, they devise their training wherever and however they can, rather than according to some rational master plan – and if the education system does not or cannot provide, private provision may grow up to do so. Whereas general streams at the post-compulsory stage are dominated by the influence of higher education, and vocational streams are often influenced by government employment and social policies, it is the technical streams which are most directly and purely influenced by the labour market. Since that is in a state of flux, it is hardly surprising that technical education is too.

Two broad themes did, however, emerge from the case studies, and the remainder of this section will deal briefly with them. The first has to do with the process of innovation in technical education, and the second with the structure of studies. It was argued above that this stream of post-compulsory education needs to respond directly to the needs of the economy and the labour market, and that the influences of the latter are often strong and direct. Several studies commented on the need for, and rapidity of, change in technical education. In France, while the mere announcement of future changes in the contents of general education arouses public disquiet, this never occurs in the same way with technical and vocational diplomas or teaching. It is true that technological change, the modification of vocational qualifications, the segmentation of the labour market, necessitate constant revision in order to match training and employment. Even in the case of technical education, changes in training are constant in each diploma course, and particularly those which lead directly into occupations which are themselves in a state of constant evolution.

However, as the Quebec study points out, the internal processes of curriculum innovation can sometimes be involved:

"The mechanism for planning and revising programmes is fairly ponderous because it involves large numbers of teachers. The co-ordinating committee for each programme is composed of delegates of the colleges which offer that programme; the co-ordinator is elected from among them. In all technical programmes, these teachers' committees are supported by industrial committees on which representatives of industry also sit. This mechanism does have the advantage of also being a means of involving the teachers themselves in the very process of change. But it can also prove slow when consensus is difficult to arrive at, and even sterile when the conflicts are irreconcilable. It is less rapid than that which is used in the Ontario CAATs, which is a real problem at a time when technological change requires profound transformations. But is that really so? Profound changes cannot be improvised; they imply the replacement of equipment and the adaptation, even the 'recycling' of teaching staff." (Country study: Quebec, Canada, pp. 30-31.)

The need for rapid innovation in technical education is leading, in the Netherlands, to a shift in the source of control:

"Reform of MBO (senior secondary vocational) curricula is progressing at a relatively slow pace and with too little involvement of employers. In order to accelerate modification of the curriculum to reflect new developments in the labour market, the number of barriers between education and industry is to be reduced by limiting the government's influence on the curriculum to determining the admission and examination requirements. This will allow changes to be made in the subject matter and didactic arrangements in MBO schools. By stating the exam syllabuses in a modular form, central government will encourage a modular presentation of subject matter; the ratio of classroom to out-of-school learning will be determined by the school." (Country study: Netherlands, p. 17.)

This theme of reducing the barriers between education and industry was evident in a number of case studies, including those for Germany, the United Kingdom and the United States. In Sweden, it also involves a shift from central to local control, and a distinction between the needs of national and local labour markets.

"The local and regional characteristics of upper secondary schooling and higher education alike have been strengthened since the end of the 1970s through the greater liberty allowed for the creation of new study programmes. These can be local follow-ons from national foundation study programmes, or else they can be alternative foundation programmes in their own right. Sometimes study programmes of this kind are also offered on a chartered basis to companies or administrative authorities. A 'twilight zone' of educational activities has evolved on the borderline between upper secondary schooling, higher education, personnel education and adult education." (Country study: Sweden, p. 38.)

The importance of education-industry links was also stressed in the Yugoslav and Italian studies. In Italy, the technical streams are the largest of the three, and the case study emphasizes the extent to which experimentation in these streams can take place without the necessity or support of a central policy; indeed the policy stalemate over the future development of post-compulsory education which has persisted for some years has not prevented a great deal of innovation in practice, such of which takes place with government support. Such innovations have been a direct response to economic and employment changes: "the development of new information technology, the rapid growth of the tertiary sector, the emergence of new models of the organisation of work". The study goes on to point out that such innovations are no longer confined to industrial fields:

> "In the technical education sector, experiments are taking place in almost all technical and professional fields. With the massive diffusion of new technologies, one can say that the demand for innovation became initially apparent above all in the industrial technical institutes... It is only during the last few years that a parallel need has shown itself in the commercial technical institutes following the development of the automation of services and the radical changes undergone by the civil service with the fiscal reforms and the impact of banking and customs changes on commercial activities." (Country study: Italy, pp. 12-13.)

There have also been changes in the structure of technical courses in several countries. In some cases, these are a response to the problem of regrouping or rationalising what had become an overly fragmented pattern. For example, the French *Baccalauréat de technicien*, introduced originally in 1969, comprised two series, F and G, which consisted of twelve and three options respectively. The projected reforms of 1986, which were not in the event implemented, envisaged regrouping these options in fewer categories, as well as reclassifying a few of them under "general" education.

The Netherlands study notes that the MBO courses are to be classified into four broad sectors (technical, commercial, agricultural and social services/health care), a reduction in the previous statutory number. In England and Wales, employment patterns also point to the need for a broader-based education in some fields:

> "Clearly, the development and increasing use of new technology is affecting the nature of employment considerably, even if in some industries and areas it is slower to arrive than was predicted in the 1970s. What is discernible is that where employers take on new staff, they expect them to be familiar with new technology and not to be limited by the boundaries of the former craft-base or narrow technical-base. Growth in employment tends to be in the service sectors, where the advance of new technology is in some cases, as in the City of London, quite dramatic. Here, too, employees and managers are expected to accept a wider brief. All this affects their skills and competence and hence their training and development needs. This is what the advent of the National Council of Vocational Qualifications (NCVQ) portends, a renewal and reorientation of vocational education to meet the needs of the 21st rather than the 19th century." (Country study: England and Wales, pp. 29-30.)

The issue of breadth versus specialisation in technical and vocational education has preoccupied planners in many countries in the last decade. As Figure 1 implies, traditional technical and vocational courses tended to end with a specific stage. But specificity implies a relatively stable and predictable labour market: one has to know what one is training for. In recent years the labour market has become much less predictable. As a consequence, some countries have moved towards the development of "occupational training families", i.e. broad groupings of previously distinct lines of study[12]. Other countries, notably those with a strong tradition of apprenticeship have retained a more specific pattern of training, partly because such training seems to equip the young person with general employment skills and attitudes, and partly because any "mismatches" between training output and labour intake seem to be accommodated by substitution among trained manpower.

The belief that the structure of employment now requires more initial breadth seems to be based on two arguments: that the organisation of work is changing, and that the very nature of work is changing. The first relates to job specifications and contracts. Whereas in the past, many jobs were relatively specific and well-defined, there appears to be a trend towards more open-ended and flexible contracts, a situation that is characteristic of Japanese employment:

"Lack of clear job demarcation has been another important characteristic of Japanese corporations. Workers are assigned to broad categories of jobs such as sales, clerical, manual, or technical positions, but corporations expect their employees to do any kind of task necessary for the work teams to accomplish certain prescribed goals. In addition, companies require their employees to perform a variety of jobs with differing work teams and in different places. Such job rotation helps firms maintain the practice of filling vacancies from within the organization and may even take place beyond the broad categories of jobs." (Country study: Japan, p. 53.)

This system reflects the predominance of internal labour markets among larger Japanese employers, and the tendency to take on employees for life, a situation which does not pertain in the less stable half of what the study characterises as a "dual economy". But the above system allows organisations to respond to rapid change:

"... [Japanese] companies diffuse concept of jobs has its own economic rationality. Some economists suggest that employment contracting on the basis of a loosely defined concept of position is favourable to the corporations. It is a way of including in any single job an infinite variation of tasks and a continuously changing situation." (Country study: Japan, p. 56.)

"... Japanese corporations have traditionally preferred hiring new graduates from schools and universities to hiring 'ready to combat' workers. New graduates are preferred because their wages are low and, more importantly, because they are presumed to have basic knowledge and flexibility, which means easy mastery of company training programmes and, consequently, reduced training costs to the employer." (Country study: Japan, p. 55.)

The Japanese case study thus exemplifies how the organisation of work can have implications for the content and structure of studies. However, one must be cautious about generalising from this example; the pattern of organisation, and the degree of job definition may vary not only from country to country but from sector to sector. Insofar as modern economies are moving towards less defined or demarcated work structures, in order to respond better to change and uncertainty, the above quotations may have a more general relevance; however, there are other important variables, such as the level of entry to the occupation, the average length of employment in a given job, and the degree of mobility among various types of workers.

The Swedish case study, however, points to a different source of change in technical education: not simply changes in the organisation of technical work, but in technology itself, leading to a veritable "Copernican revolution" in training. For example, the study cites the integration of production and maintenance in the electrical field, and describes a more general shift towards organising technical work on the basis of functions rather than occupations or sectors:

"The pre-existing skills profile for monitoring, controlling and servicing equipment in power plants and ships is well suited to the modern industrial environment. This line, unlike traditional vocational education, trains students for functions, not industrial sectors. A great many of these functional skills are common to numerous industries and workplaces, whatever their productive specialities. Students acquire a peripheral competence which is common to many duties surrounding the specific core skills. Hitherto the division of labour between vocational training in schools and the employment sector respectively has been such that core skills have formed the basis on which the lines of upper secondary school were defined, whereas peripheral competence has been supplied in the form of personnel training for skilled workers... The solution represented by the Production and Maintenance Engineering line makes a secondary school primarily responsible for peripheral competence, with companies taking over a larger share of core skills." (Country study: Sweden, p. 32.)

Another way of interpreting this shift from "core" to "peripheral" competence is to distinguish between four elements in any technology: element, process, control, and environment. All technologies involve elements, usually materials such as metals, plastics, organisms or fluids. All technologies involve the interaction or transformation of such elements, through various processes – physical, chemical, electrical, biological, etc. – or combinations of these. The processing of the elements is subject to control, and takes place in a certain environment. The multiplicity of elements and processes creates a great diversity of technologies, and leads to the many often quite separate lines of study in traditional technical education. What seems to be happening now is that the third and fourth aspects of technology listed above – control and environment – are becoming relatively more important. Control, in particular, has a homogenizing effect on technology, because of the generic nature of information processing and system design. This does not of course mean that the diversity of elements and processes disappears, but that it is to some extent subsumed under a more general pattern of control. And with the increasing automation of various processes, whether mechanical, electrical, or other, the technician is now less concerned with the direct manipulation of elements and processes, and exercises a more indirect role, in monitoring and modifying the overall control system.

This change has three consequences for technical education. First, as the Swedish study notes, it may alter the relationship between pre-employment and on-the-job training. Pre-employment technical education increasingly concentrates on the generic control functions, leaving the specific skills related to elements and processes to be acquired as necessary on the job. Secondly, because the control and environmental aspects of technology are less heterogeneous and more generalised than elements and processes, it becomes possible to group technical courses more broadly than in the past, when they were primarily defined in terms of their specific element/process interaction. Thirdly, the balance between manipulative and cognitive skills tilts towards the latter, since whereas elements and processes typically require manipulation (often to a high degree of precision) control involves the processing of information. It is the equipment itself which now provides the precision. Technicians therefore need to be competent in surveillance, error-tracing, adaptive programming, and system analysis. And with the increasingly powerful and systemic nature of technologies, they need to be much more aware of environmental impacts and side-effects than before, not only in the nuclear field, but in agriculture, health, transport and many others. Given all these demands, it is hardly surprising that technicians are increasingly being trained at the post-secondary level in some countries.

This kind of argument should not be pushed too far. There remain many technologies where the technician is still directly involved with specific elements and processes, and as suggested in Chapter II, the analysis needs to go beyond broad generalisations about sectors, to a more precise investigation of changes in particular occupations. Another question that needs to be considered is how such an analysis can apply to "non-material" technologies, where the "elements" are people, money, or information, and the "processes" are behavioural and social rather than physical or chemical. We noted above that the term "technician" sounds rather odd applied to such cases. The elements have a life of their own, and the processes are often ill-defined. Can a hotel or a bank, for example, be described in technological terms? The whole impact of technological innovation on service sector occupations has major implications for education and training, which deserve careful analysis. It is not easy to generalise in this field, first because the timing of the impact of technology differs from occupation to occupation (some occupations, such as financial services, seem closer to the epicentre of innovation than others, such as publishing), and secondly because the nature of that impact may go through several stages, for example, initially creating jobs, and then replacing them. In others again, such as health, the interaction between people and equipment is crucial, and advanced technology can coexist with relatively primitive forms of organisation and communication.

Finally, it should be noted that these changes in the nature of technology itself affect the relationship between different types or streams of post-compulsory education. In the past, it was often the emphasis on theory that distinguished technical from vocational streams. Thus it is possible for someone with a "vocational" training to be *more* skilled in terms of craft and manipulation than a technician in the same field; what the latter had, however, was a better understanding of the theoretical principles involved in the processing of the elements. Any change in the technology itself is bound to affect this distinction. A shift of emphasis towards "control" could lead to a greater emphasis on "theory" in vocational courses than hitherto, thus weakening the distinction between "craft" and "technician". On the other hand, the shift towards "control" could lead to a quantum jump in the theoretical requirements of technician occupations, as they deal less with discrete processes, and more with total systems. This would tend to elevate technician courses to the level of higher or post-secondary education. The evidence from the case studies seems to be that both these trends exist in various countries. It should also be remembered that the definition of technician (and those who teach them) is partly a social definition. Indeed, in France there are clear differences in title and status among the various types of post-compulsory teachers, and moves have been made over a period of years to bring these closer together.

Unlike general streams, technical education does not have a fixed external point of reference in higher education. Unlike vocational education, the subject of the next section, it has not typically been the object of major policy initiatives in recent years. Indeed, in some cases it has been difficult to define at all, squeezed between the more palpable entities of "general" and "vocational". Whatever the importance of technical *streams*, however, there can be no doubt about the importance of technical *education*, and its close links with technological innovation. There are indeed reasons for thinking that it may become more, not less, central to post-compulsory education in the future, reasons which will be spelled out towards the end of the report. Next, however, we must turn our attention to the third of the broad types of education that have emerged by the post-compulsory stage, namely short-cycle *vocational* courses which prepare for skilled or semi-skilled jobs, or, in some case, no job at all.

4. Vocational education

Vocational education, in the OECD typology, refers broadly to short-cycle post-compulsory courses which lead to semi-skilled or skilled jobs in any of the three main sectors of employment. In terms of educational and employment status vocational courses often come lower in the pecking order, though as we shall see, their status depends on various factors and varies not only from course to course but from country to country. Three initial points should be made about vocational education.

First, whereas general and technical streams are typically characterised by a single mode of study (school/college-based, full-time) there are two main modes of study in vocational education: full-time and part-time, and as the statistics in Chapter III show, the balance of these varies from country to country. In fact, the essential curricular difference lies not in the time, but the locus of studies. In some countries, all or nearly all the training is carried out in schools or colleges, off the job, whereas in others, much of it takes place in employment, on the job. Thus the so-called part-timer may be learning just as much, though in a different way, as the full-timer; a point which is particularly important in "dual" systems.

Secondly, it is this sector of post-compulsory education which has above all been faced with the problem of youth unemployment. Although unemployment has affected young people in all educational and occupational categories, the general evidence is that the fewer or lower the educational qualifications one has, the less likely one is to find a job. The concept of vocation traditionally implies work, whether in employment or self-employment; the absence of employment therefore affects the basic rationale of vocational courses.

Thirdly, in some countries vocational streams are now providing for groups of young people for whom they never catered before. While all post-compulsory streams have experienced quantitative changes, vocational streams have perhaps experienced a greater qualitative change in the kind of student they provide for than the other streams. To the "traditional" vocational student must now be added young people who in previous years would perhaps have gone directly into the labour market. And it is worth pointing out that if there is a high drop-out rate among such students, the labour markets that used to absorb them were also characterised by instability and discontinuity. Perhaps those secondary labour markets have now been replaced by a secondary "education market", which has some similarities.

As with the other main sub-divisions of post-compulsory education, the authors responded to three main questions. Since in this case the questions related to quite different aspects of vocational education, they will be taken one by one. However, before doing so, there is one important issue which although not pinpointed by a question, was nevertheless of common concern: the educational and employment *status* of vocational education.

It is striking that several studies mentioned the creation, or planned creation, of new vocational *qualifications*. In France, in addition to the existing *Certificat d'aptitude professionnelle* (CAP) and *Brevet d'études professionnelles* (BEP), a new *Baccalauréat professionnel* was created in 1985. This involves two years further study on top of the BEP. To date, it has enrolled just over 8 000 students, and its role in the system is too new to comment on. In Italy a higher vocational qualification (the *Maturità professionale*) which builds on existing vocational qualifications has been established. In both countries, the choice of the title seems to imply a certain parity with general qualifications at this stage, and such qualifications also give formal access to higher education. In the United Kingdom, the new two-year Youth Training Scheme will lead to a formal qualification; in addition, the new Certificate of Pre-Vocational Education has been established in England and Wales, and in Scotland a new National Certificate has now replaced most pre-existing non-advanced vocational qualifications, though equivalences with older qualifications still exist. (It should however be said that the main emphasis in the United Kingdom at present is on rationalising existing vocational qualifications rather than creating new ones). In Quebec, there is a proposal to create both a new *Diplôme* and *Certificat d'études professionnelles* (DEP and CEP), which would normally be completed by the ages of 17 and 18.

There are various reasons behind the creation of new vocational qualifications, but in some cases at least, the need to raise the perceived status of such streams and courses seems to be an important one. Several studies referred to the status of staff in vocational education, and described attempts to raise this to the level of the staff in technical and general education. And the Swedish study noted that the timetabling of vocational courses had been altered to make them comparable with other lines.

Such measures raise fundamental questions about the status of vocational education which are difficult to answer. Are we talking about status in the eyes of employers, educators or students? Is the perception of status similar among all three? What criteria are implied in judgements of status? Educational level? Employment level? Wider social or moral criteria? And if status is a relative or positional phenomenon, surely some courses are always going to be lower in the pecking order than others? Is educational status ultimately a reflection of social status? Such questions cannot be properly explored here, but perhaps one point can be made. As long as there is a single pecking order in education or employment, status differences are inevitable, and are not going to be altered by merely cosmetic changes in labels and titles. However, where there are multiple status hierarchies (i.e. several kinds of pecking order) involving different kinds of criteria, courses are more likely to be seen as "different" rather than "unequal". The inclusion of all forms of post-compulsory education and training in a single institutional, administrative and certificatory framework may reinforce the single hierarchy, if such a hierarchy ultimately embodies a single set of values. In the education system, such values tend to reflect the dominant values of higher education, as the apex of the system; hence the emphasis is placed on theory, abstraction and cognitive-intellectual ability. Within such a single hierarchy, vocational education cannot easily raise its status, because it tends to rate low on such measures.

However, where post-compulsory education has developed multiple institutional forms, there may be a greater diversity of values, and a plurality of hierarchies. This seems to be more the case in the German and Swiss systems, where the apprenticeship-based vocational streams are well regarded *in their own right*. Ultimately, their social and employment status may be lower than that of the general and technical streams, but the fact that in Germany one quarter of all *Abiturienten* (*Gymnasium* school-leavers) aimed at getting an apprenticeship place in 1986 speaks for itself. This is not because students see apprenticeship as a means of progressing to higher education (though some do progress) but because the apprenticeship has its own status in its own terms, and has a secure social, occupational and indeed educational role. (Apprenticeship in Germany has long been seen as a means of moral and civic education, as well as leading to the acquisition of knowledge and skills). The Swiss study describes measures designed to encourage apprentices to attend higher vocational schools, in order to deepen their understanding of the theoretical aspects of their work, and progress to higher qualifications.

The issue of status creates a policy dilemma. Some countries have in recent years attempted to create a more comprehensive or at least integrated pattern of post-compulsory education, partly in order to raise the status of vocational courses and give students on them the opportunity to progress or transfer to higher levels. For example, this has been the case in Norway, where such policies may be judged to have had some success in this respect, and is clearly one aim of policies in Quebec, Yugoslavia and Greece. The perception of status is contingent upon not only educational variables (such as the role and breadth of general streams, and the extent to which they are identified with access to higher education), but wider social ones, such as wages and salary differentials, and the general attribution of status in the culture. Where such variables favour egalitarian policies, a comprehensive or integrated approach to post-compulsory education may become well established, and in time form part of the institutional structures which reinforce that perception. However, such a policy may equally reduce the existing plurality of values and criteria at the post-compulsory stage to a single hierarchy which is dominated, in the end, by higher education. The net effect then is to lower the status of courses which do not best represent those values, i.e. precisely those vocational courses the policy was meant to benefit. This assumes, of course, that higher education does embody a single set of cognitive-intellectual values, but higher education is itself more plural and diverse in some countries than others. For example, in the United States, the diversity of higher education, and in particular the existence of the community colleges, seems to allow a more plural set of educational criteria to exist, a fact perhaps reflected in the wider use of the term "post-secondary" there. And the U.S. study also describes the rapid growth of employment-based studies (dubbed "corporate classrooms" in the book by N. P. Eurich)[13], which are coming to constitute a "third leg" of the education system, and which seem likely to further pluralise educational values and criteria.

The first case study question had to do with the scope and structure of vocational courses:

> Has the trend been towards broader vocational courses (occupational training families, generic skills) or more specific courses (sub-skills, modular training)?

The reasoning behind the question has already been spelled out in the section on technical education: change and uncertainty in the labour market may require a broader, more polyvalent training base. Yet again, the reality is not quite so straightforward. It is true that the two countries which have the largest percentage of the age group in apprenticeships at this stage reported decreases in the number of specific apprenticeship/training lines: Germany from 600 in 1972 to 429 in 1985, and Switzerland from 400 to 360 in recent years. (The Swiss system has retained a more specialised pattern for reasons spelled out in that case study.) Some of the reduction can be explained by the virtual disappearance of some traditional, highly-specialised crafts, but there has also been a definite trend towards more generic courses: for example, in Germany, from 42 to 6 industrial metalwork lines. This trend has been based on the concept of *Stufenausbildung* (training by stages) in which the first year of apprenticeship provides a foundation for several lines and the subsequent years become more specific. As the study notes, this can be done most effectively by large firms, but small firms have also established joint workshops in order to provide apprentices with a broader, initial base.

In other countries, there were examples of both specific and generic approaches, as for example in England and Wales:

> "TVEI (Technical and Vocational Education Initiative) is a 14-18 programme, aimed mainly at schools and increasingly committed to the principles of *Better Schools*. Its target is the attainment of recognised vocational qualifications. CPVE (Certificate of Pre-Vocational Education) has a complex design involving a compulsory core, various modules and additional studies. It is aimed at young, potential school-leavers who are uncommitted and it offers them a broad-based one-year generic course in occupational skills blended with general education. This gives young people a basis on which to progress into a range of vocational education provision in which they can refine those skills into more occupationally-specific areas. YTS on the other hand offers young people the basis of acquiring over two years significant experience of work, some quite specific occupational skills which they may then use to gain employment or (less frequently) in setting up their own enterprises. (Only approximately 50% of YTS trainees obtain immediate employment on completion of training.) One of the problems of YTS in particular is the uneasy balance between the scheme being a political measure to adjust youth unemployment on the one hand, and it being a long overdue renewal of the

country's bad track-record in vocational training on the other. This uneasy coalescence of origins and interpretations still plagues the scheme. Assuming that the renewal of training is the key and lasting motive behind YTS, then the model appears to be to give young people from 16-17 an opportunity to explore, experience and gain generic skills in a range of occupational competences. From 17-19 the expectation is that they will focus on a more specific occupational skill basis. This seems to be an assumption and model that also underpin the 14-18 TVEI scheme, although so far the output from TVEI has been so small that generalisations are difficult." (Country study: England and Wales, pp. 31-32.)

Two points are worth noting: first the fact that the TVEI scheme crosses the compulsory/post-compulsory line; and secondly, the reference to self-employment as well as employment, which reflects current United Kingdom government policy, and is an emphasis that is found in a number of Member countries, particularly in Europe. In the past, the implicit assumption of most vocational education has been that the young person would "find employment". It is difficult to know exactly how far this assumption permeated the content and process of courses. The core skills needed for either employment or self-employment in a given occupation may be much the same. However, whereas the employed person will need to know about working in and for an organisation, the self-employed person will need different *adjunct* skills to do with finance, marketing, legal requirements, and general self-management. But the difference between employment and self-employment may affect the process and ethos of courses more, and more subtly. Self-employment requires autonomy, initiative and an accurate perception of risk, and while such qualities are not necessarily absent in the employed person, they are likely to be less salient.

The Japanese study, however, links the more recent decline in the status of vocational courses there to a shift in the perception of self-employment. It should be noted that although such courses can be regarded as "vocational" in terms of their intake and occupational outlets, they nevertheless share some of the characteristics of "technical" streams in terms of their format (three-year full-time) and content (which includes some general education). Indeed, the separate development of such courses out of the post-World War II comprehensive system in the 1950s was motivated not only by the need to replenish their staff and equipment but also by the desire of some people in that field to preserve the independent value or ethos of vocational/technical education. In the 1960s, the status of vocational courses was relatively high, and this status was connected with certain employment expectations:

"This career orientation towards self-employed status was an important part of the ethos which sustained the heydays of upper secondary vocational courses. In 1966, an American economist administered a questionnaire survey to approximately 7 000 male upper secondary students and their fathers, with a view to finding the key to Japan's rapid economic growth through analysing youths' career choices. She found that vocational course students' image of the ideal occupational career was achieving self-employed status after accumulating various experiences at small or medium-sized firms." (Country study: Japan, p. 51.)

However, expectations have now changed:

"Despite the fact that the objective chances of achieving the status of self-employed have remained rather stable, upper secondary vocational students and their parents have lost their taste for independent work, as they grew accustomed to working for big firms and expecting to lead stable careers there. But it was also clear that in the large corporate bureaucracies possession of a university diploma was much more favourable than an upper secondary certificate. This was one of the reasons why vocational courses have become less popular than academic/general courses since the mid-60s." (Country study: Japan, p. 52.)

The issue of breadth versus specialisation cannot be left with some analysis of the concept of polyvalence. The concepts of polyvalence and generic skills have been widely discussed in recent years, particularly in the European context[14]. The current emphasis on "basic skills" in the United States seems to be partly of the same kind and for the same reason: the need to prepare young people for a demanding and fast-changing labour market. If one assumes that the labour market at this level is indeed more uncertain and unstable than it used to be, does it follow that broad-based courses are the best preparation for it? The answer depends on two things: an analysis of the kinds of behaviours that are needed in the current job market; and an analysis of how knowledge and skills are transferred from one situation to another.

To take the latter first: there are broadly speaking two different models of transfer of learning. The first, deriving from behavioural psychology, sees transfer as largely dependent on the situation. If there are identical elements of content or procedure in two situations, what was learned or applied in the first is likely to be transferred and applied to the second. The second model is associated with cognitive or information-processing models of psychology, and views transfer as largely dependent on the person. If a person employs strategic or generalised habits of thinking and analysis, transfer is likely to occur; if, on the other hand, he or she tends to conceive of each situation or problem as specific or unique, little transfer will take place. The implication of the latter view is that the predisposition to transfer can to some extent be encouraged through for example giving the student tasks which demand transfer, and also developing a positive attitude to flexibility and risk-taking. "Teaching for transfer" therefore involves not only cognition, but also attitudes and self-concept. However, it may be that the very concept of transfer is inappropriate. The idea of transfer implies the existence of two distinct and specific task situations, but the issue may be better understood in terms of a general *relativising* of constructs and approaches of the kind that a general education may accomplish. It is not so much a question of learning to transfer something from Task A to Task B as approaching all such tasks from a relativised and analytic perspective, of the kind described for example by Perry in his studies of cognitive development[15].

All models of transfer, however, stress a solid initial foundation. Unless the original procedure or skill is well learned, indeed "over-learned", it is not likely to be transferable, because it will not have been thoroughly integrated into the person's cognitive and behavioural repertoire. However, the objective possibilities of transfer depend also on the nature of the tasks involved. It was suggested in the section on technical education that there are certain unifying or homogenising trends in technology itself, related to the growing importance of control systems. At the vocational level, this may be less true, since semi-skilled or skilled jobs are more likely to involve discrete elements and processes rather than generic control, which is a higher order function. However, the structure of tasks in employment is also a matter not only of elements and processes but of economics. In the past, for example, the car worker might well have been able to carry out a range of related tasks, but would not have been allowed to do so, because of strict job demarcation. In other words, the modern trend towards "multi-skilling" at this level of industrial work may be due less to changes in the content of labour, than its organisation.

The above analysis may help to explain why different countries seem to have adopted different vocational strategies in terms of specific or generic skills. The emphasis on broad-based courses, occupational training families, generic skills and general education which one finds in some countries or sectors contrasts with the adherence to more traditional, specific patterns of training in others, notably in those with strong apprenticeship systems. On the face of it, the latter would seem to be dysfunctional in an unpredictable labour market. However, the evidence seems to be that they continue to function well, and this may be for several reasons. First, they provide the solid basis in certain skills which are the prerequisite of any transfer. Secondly, the skills they include are to some extent inherently transferable: after all, many jobs involve work with machines, money, people or information. But thirdly, they provide a generic training in the processes of work: time-keeping, planning, searching, checking, decision-making, co-operation with others, and so forth. So although they may be relatively specific in terms of work *content*, they are generic in terms of work *process*. By contrast, the broad-based courses may give a wider basis in content, but provide a less thorough training in the processes of work.

Finally, one must not underestimate the capacity and opportunities people have to continue learning on the job. One of the hazards of concentrating on formal education and training is the disregard of non-formal or informal learning. Whatever kind of initial, formal vocational education people receive, they can usually complement this, or compensate for this, by on-the-job learning, both individually and collectively. Thus the exact structure and content of post-compulsory vocational education, though important, may be less irrevocable than policy-makers sometimes suppose, because working life in many jobs constitutes a continual correction and adaptation of initial knowledge and skills. Indeed one of the hidden tragedies of unemployment is that it withdraws from people not only the opportunity to work, but the opportunity to learn.

The second question about vocational streams follows on naturally from the above discussion:

> To what extent do vocational streams emphasize non-cognitive aspects such as attitudes, social skills or work norms? Has the emphasis on work-based or school/college-based vocational education changed?

As some of the authors pointed out, the question is itself revealing. Why this emphasis on attitudes and norms only in vocational education streams? Why not in technical and general education as well? The point is well taken. It is generally assumed that attitudes and norms are less of a problem in the latter; that the problems of socialisation and alienation are most prominent in vocational courses. The most obvious, though not only, indicator of this problem is drop-out. This was an issue which was referred to in all the studies, but in particular those from Italy, Quebec, Sweden, the United States and Yugoslavia. The U.S. study includes a detailed discussion of drop-out trends, and the state and federal measures which are being taken to counteract it. While drop-out or wastage is thus obviously a matter of common concern, it is not easy to consider it in isolation from all the other issues in this study. Any analysis of drop-out quickly leads back to the main elements of provision – the content and structure of courses, the teaching style, the institutional ethos, the prospects of employment, and so on – with which this study is concerned, and it therefore seems better to consider it as an aspect of each of these, rather than as a separate topic. But there can be no doubt that the phenomenon of drop-out relates closely to the issues of student motivation and socialisation. all the other issues in this study. Any analysis of drop-out quickly leads back to the main elements of provision – the content and structure of courses, the teaching style, the institutional ethos, the prospects of employment, and so on – with which this study is concerned, and it therefore seems better to consider it as an aspect of each of these, rather than as a separate topic. But there can be no doubt that the phenomenon of drop-out relates closely to the issues of student motivation and socialisation.

All education involves socialisation i.e. induction into the norms and patterns of society. However, the nature and process of socialisation varies from stage to stage and sector to sector.

Much of the socialisation that takes place in the primary or lower secondary school is either general in nature, or a socialisation into schooling itself. By the post-compulsory stage, however, the process of socialisation has become more differentiated and specific, anticipating the social and occupational destinations of students. The pre-academic streams anticipate the culture of higher education; the technical streams may embody a kind of intermediate culture; and vocational streams prepare young people, affectively as well as cognitively, for skilled or semi-skilled work[16]. There are of course complexities, tensions and ambiguities within each of these. The fact that socialisation is a more overt theme in vocational streams than the others does not mean that it does not occur in pre-academic and technical education, merely that it often is less effective: students are less willing to identify with their anticipated role. And as the Scottish study points out, there is sometimes an unwillingness even to recognise this dimension of education:

"With respect to work norms and (especially) attitudes the explicit philosophy is more ambivalent, partly because of doubts about the ability of the formal curriculum to influence them, but mainly because attempts to influence attitudes are widely regarded as incompatible with educational principles. The hidden curriculum of vocational education, and especially YTS, is a subject of vigorous debate. Critics of the 'new vocationalism' represent it as an illiberal attempt to prepare young people ideologically for a world of unemployment and unfulfilling work, and to inhibit their development of a critical understanding of this world. Others question whether this tendency is in fact new, and suggest that because the objectives and outcomes of both YTS and modules are more tightly specified they are, by the same token, more clearly delimited. One consequence of modularisation may be to inhibit the part played by colleges in occupational socialisation, since students are less likely to belong to a stable student group and are more likely to be taught alongside students preparing for different occupations." (Country study: Scotland, pp. 31-32.)

The Japanese study comments on what appears to be an overt, rather than hidden, affective aspect of the curriculum for all streams at the post-compulsory stage:

"Parents, children and teachers believe that it is not innate ability (expressed by IQ scores), but the amount of effort invested that determines academic results. Teachers seize every opportunity to emphasize the importance of effort, and parents co-operate with schools in urging their children to study. This ethic of effortism, as it were, seems closely related to the fact that school curricula and test problems have historically been organized so that average pupils can keep up only if they make great efforts (for example, spend much time in rote memorizing)." (Country study: Japan, p. 27.)

This emphasis on effort occurs not only at entry to the lower secondary and upper secondary levels; it can also be seen in relation to recuitment into private companies or government agencies. In particular, students in the post-compulsory vocational streams are strongly encouraged to make every effort to acquire various occupational certificates. This is not to help such students get the relevant jobs, but in order that they should lead diligent lives and add to their chances of being employed through having a record of, or at least giving the impression of, diligence.

It is important to recognise that the "non-cognitive" aspects of education can also refer to personal qualities and personal motivation, as well as general or specific socialisation, and several studies mentioned these. But the question implicitly linked the issue of socialisation with the location or setting of education in either the educational institution or the workplace. Thus, in France, the development of vocational education has been concerned not only with the content of courses, but also non-cognitive competences. That is to say the accent has been placed equally on behaviour and "savoir-être" in the world of work and in social life. These new emphases have become apparent particularly in the increasingly frequent introduction of training placements or stages in the workplace. This has in fact been a more general trend for some years in both training establishments and firms. On taking office, in the spring of 1986, the new administration underlined the need to strengthen the links between education and industry. The main measures envisage the encouragement of reciprocal mobility between education and industrial personnel. It is interesting that in France, as in some other countries, the relationship between institution and workplace is seen not only in terms of students but also staff.

As was noted earlier, the balance of emphasis on institution-based or work-based learning reflects history as well as policy. Two countries in particular (Germany and Switzerland) have strong traditions of apprenticeship allied to vocational school provision: the "dual system". The Swiss study distinguished further between four different types of apprenticeship: traditional craft; industrial; modern craft (combining elements of the first two); and commercial/technical, which tends to have a larger off-the-job element. There is not room here to discuss these four types in detail, but the case study is a valuable reminder that apprenticeship is not a static, but evolving and flexible, form of training. Indeed, it is interesting that both policy and demand have combined in the Netherlands to increase sharply the number of apprenticeships in recent years, from over 21 000 in 1983 to over 57 000 in 1985. In other countries, the number of apprenticeships has declined with the decline of traditional industries, while in others again, such as the United States, they play a small but important role in supplying skilled labour.

The general arguments in favour of institution-based or work-based vocational training are well known and need only be noted briefly here. Institution-based training in schools and colleges should provide coherent and intensive courses which cover both the practical and the increasingly important theoretical elements in either specific jobs or broader job groups. Such courses can be planned and evaluated systematically, and taught by trained teachers. On the other hand, work-based training promises a relevant and practical training in a "real" work environment, under the supervision of skilled workers with whose role the young person can identify, and often with the benefit of up-to-date equipment. In addition, the main costs are borne by the employer, who also gets some benefit from having an increasingly skilled employee. Whereas institution-based training is sometimes criticised for being costly, dated, theoretical and artificial, work-based training is sometimes attacked for being narrow, variable in quality, poorly organised and taught, and a source of cheap labour.

The case studies point to some convergence between the two. For example, some of the institution-based vocational lines in Swedish upper secondary schools now incorporate work placements, often in the second year, and there are plans to add a third, practical year to some two-year lines. In Quebec, which is also firmly wedded to an "institutional" model of training, the use of work placements is also being explored and extended. In both countries, the motivating effect on students of working in a "real" work environment seems to be one factor in the change; access to modern equipment, often the Achilles heel of schools and colleges, is another. Employers also get to know, and may retain, some of the trainees sent to them. By contrast, some apprentices now spend much of their early training not in the workplace itself, but in training workshops attached to the company, or to a group of companies. Here the main considerations seem to be cost and safety: it is unwise to let raw apprentices loose on expensive and sometimes dangerous modern technology. It may be therefore that over a period of years, the two distinct patterns of vocational training will become less so, as the advantages and constraints of each become more widely recognised.

The final question under the heading of vocational education was as follows:

What kind of educational or counselling provision is made for young people who have a high risk of being unemployed, or are disadvantaged in other ways?

It should be noted first of all that the percentage of the age group at risk from unemployment varies greatly from country to country (see Table 2, Chapter III) from under 1 per cent to over 33 per cent in 1985. The scale of unemployment has an obvious bearing on policy: one might expect that where it is a relatively minor problem, it would be coped with by marginal changes in existing provision, and where it is a major problem, entire new programmes would have to be set in place. But it must also be remembered that youth unemployment within the aggregate figure may be sharply concentrated in certain groups, regions or locations (e.g. inner city).

Almost all the studies made some reference to special provision for "risk" groups, and the United States study discusses this problem and the related one of illiteracy in some detail. The nature of provision described by the case studies varies greatly. In some countries, the measures are aimed at modifying and extending *existing* provision to cope with such groups, rather than creating separate or special programmes: this seem to be the general strategy in Japan, Quebec, Switzerland, Yugoslavia and Germany, although the "foundation-year" schemes (BGJ and BVJ) in the last country seem partly to fulfill a recuperative role. This is also the case in the United Kingdom in the sense that the Youth Training Scheme has grown rapidly to cater for a large percentage of the age group (about 50 per cent of school-leavers), including those who in previous years might have directly entered employment; and recently announced policies are likely to increase this to include virtually all young people who are not in employment or full-time education. A number of countries have, however, created special measures or programmes to cope with the problem. Here, one should mention the development of non-formal education in the Netherlands in which "activities are geared to helping young people to cope with the problems of everyday life"; various measures in France, including short (3 to 6-month) modular programmes involving work experience, training and counselling; and various measures in the United States targeted particularly at disadvantaged ethnic groups. The U.S. study describes a wide range of both state and federal programmes designed to help those who are deemed to be at risk. The main issues in Federal programmes are how to "generate the skills and motivation necessary for success in education beyond high school and how to overcome the financial pressures of continuing in high school and progressing to post-secondary education", and there appears to be a greater emphasis than before on preventing drop-out before it happens, rather than attempting to remedy it after it has. This leads to a search for indicators which will help to predict drop-out, such as poor academic performance, discipline problems or family difficulties, factors which tend to interact rather than operate in isolation from one another.

While the policies aimed at risk groups vary from country to country, certain common themes emerged from the case studies. There seems to an increasing involvement on the part of government ministries beyond education, perhaps reflecting a less purely "educational" view of such risks; in particular labour and welfare ministries seem to be playing a greater role. This is a recognition that motivation and socialisation at the post-compulsory stage involve a mixture of educational, occupational and social factors. There is also a greater involvement of the private sector in some countries, with government funds being channelled indirectly through employers or community agencies, rather being used directly to set up government education or training programmes. This reflects a more general trend towards a public-private mix of provision at the post-compulsory stage in some countries. Thirdly, there is a tendency in some Member countries to tackle these problems at the level of the region (e.g. state, locality) rather than on a national scale. The United States study emphasizes the role of the states in such provision, and it is perhaps to be expected in countries which have federal or regional structures, such as Germany, Italy, Switzerland and Yugoslavia. But it is worth noting that in Sweden, a country with strong traditions of central provision, municipal programmes have grown up to form what is virtually a parallel system:

> "Different measures to meet youth unemployment materialised in municipal youth centres, which took over responsibility for the 'marginal groups'. Two different upper secondary systems with different organisation, scope and content have thus emerged. The municipal youth centres have a kind of 'rehabilitation ethos', where the individual pupil's interests always have priority. Integrated upper secondary school represents a mix of academic/school/working-life ethos, where credential goals are balanced against pupil aptitudes. In order to bring closer together upper secondary schools and municipal programmes to combat youth unemployment, the National Board of Education recommended that, as from the 1986/87 school year, individual contracts should be drawn up with all participants in these programmes. A principle of this kind is currently being applied." (Country study: Sweden, pp. 7-8.)

The examples cited above serve to raise three questions about the "risk groups". First, are the needs of such groups better met by extending existing programmes or creating special ones? Special programmes may meet their needs more flexibly, but their very distinctness can stigmatise the young people they enrol. Secondly, what is the optimum balance between direct state provision, and indirect government support for private sector developments? Clearly the answer to this question will reflect more general social and economic policies, but there seems to be more emphasis on the potential role of the private sector in several countries, even to the point of the "privatisation" of some provision. Thirdly, what is the optimum balance between central and local provision? Underlying this question is the distinction between national and local labour markets, an aspect explored in the Swedish study. Semi-skilled employment is associated with local labour markets, in which connections, references and self-presentation may be as important as formal qualifications. Should training schemes for the risk groups therefore be planned in terms of local labour markets? This might make sense, and seems to be a trend in several countries. But training policy will in this respect mirror general employment policies, and there is a danger of locking young people into declining industries and even regions.

The final point to be made about the "risk groups" is more abstract but nonetheless important, and it has to do with attribution. Phrases like "risk group", or "marginal group" appear to attribute the risk or marginality to the group. Their situation seems to be a consequence of their attributes. However, one can just as well argue that their attributes are a consequence of their situation: it is not they who have created their marginality, but the employment situation which has imposed marginality upon them. It is easy to move from concepts such as "marginal group" to policies which are built on the assumption that the problem or deficit lies in the person, not the situation. Twenty years ago, when youth unemployment was minimal in most OECD countries, there was of course talk of "youth culture" and the "generation gap", but that is not the same as marginality. The prime change has been not in the young people themselves (despite arguments about standards of achievement and attitudes) but in the economic and employment situation. Despite the current emphasis in many countries on the need for basic skills, the U.S. study cited one piece of research which suggests that employers do not in fact screen job applicants carefully for basic skills, and rely more on standard educational qualifications. These are, in their use if not always their design, norm-referenced: they function to sort people in situations of scarcity. In fact, much screening for employment relies on such indirect or surrogate measures, mainly for reasons of cost and convenience. The assumption that young people cannot get jobs because they lack basic skills needs to be empirically tested; because "lack of skills" can simply be a rationalisation of lack of jobs.

The last question about vocational streams also referred to counselling. Again, one may ask why this issue was raised specifically in relation to the risk groups, and not for example in technical or general education; and again, the point is well taken. As was stressed in a previous report on *Education and Training after Basic Schooling*, the post-compulsory stage, for all young people, is a stage of allocation and choice, and hence requires a particular emphasis on guidance and counselling. Guidance and counselling is a specialist field, and this study did not attempt to deal with it in any detail. The responses to the question varied. Several were critical of the provision of counselling in their system; in other countries (e.g. Switzerland) it appeared to function effectively. It is difficult to generalise, but one can at least point to the importance of this topic not only for professional counsellors, but for *teachers*. Teachers and work supervisors often provide the first or front line of guidance at the post-compulsory stage, as a natural extension of their teaching or supervisory role, and students often gravitate towards those who can advise them informally in this way. However, the help they give is usually based more on natural aptitude and inclination than systematic knowledge or training. As the England/Wales and other studies imply, the training of post-compulsory teachers, and others who have comparable responsibilities, needs to take this adjunct or extended role into account[17]:

> "Alongside and within the pre-vocational provision in every case is the requirement for educational, personal and career counselling. It is interesting to note that the emphasis is stronger in this sector than in almost any other. Clearly one of the reasons for this is that young people who, say, ten years ago would have expected to obtain employment are now expected to be enthused to continue learning. Thus counselling can be used to 'cool out' and deal with the antagonism that many will feel towards more education or training. Clearly some of the growth in counselling provision has been due to this reason. A less cynical and more optimistic view is that pre-vocational education is about transition: to motivate young people to learn through building on the sense of purpose they can achieve through work. In this case counselling skills are likely to be necessary for all the adults, teachers and supervisors involved in such schemes. Also, if the potential of the changing system is to provide more links and routes through which the young person may progress, perhaps via a variety of different modules at different levels, then access to good quality mediated information is vital. Thus the process of educational and vocational guidance becomes an essential element of the provision, not just for pre-vocational but for vocational and general education as well." (Country study: England and Wales, pp. 34-35.)

There was not time, unfortunately, to explore the issues of information, guidance and counselling further in this study, but their importance for the post-compulsory stage cannot be doubted.

V

CONTENT, PROCESS AND STRUCTURE

1. The content of courses

The main focus of this report is the organisation and content of studies at the post-compulsory stage: the curriculum. And yet much of the time has been spent, unavoidably, discussing everything that surrounds the curriculum – institutional structures, access, qualifications, employment and so on – rather than the topic itself. This chapter will therefore directly address some issues to do with what is taught, how, and in what form: the content, process and structure of studies.

As curriculum theorists point out, these three aspects of studies are intimately linked, and one cannot be analysed without reference to the others. In particular, it is not enough simply to analyse content. Content has to be covered. But what do we mean by "covered"? It is all very well to say that the student must learn or know something, but what kind of learning or knowing? Being able to reproduce something is not the same as being able to apply or analyse it: and these distinctions are linked to concepts of "level" and "progression" in education. Level is not only a matter of the scope but of the type of learning; and the higher the level, the more complex the types of knowing and learning, until one is asking the student to engage in sophisticated behaviours such as interpretation, problem-solving or even problem-posing[18].

All this takes place not on paper, not in some abstract educational void, but in actual institutions with real timetables, teachers, students and facilities. The content of courses is mediated through processes; indeed, one can say, paradoxically, that the teachers and teaching methods, and the general environment of the course also constitute a kind of "content": they are part of the totality experienced by the student. Likewise, the content of a course exists within a certain format or structure, which reflects the structures of formal education, and in particular the structure of assessment and qualifications. Such structures "frame" the content in both obvious and subtle ways, and indeed the concept of "non-formal" education refers less to differences in content, than to differences in the style, form and content of education[19].

What issues relate to the content of post-compulsory education and training? Clearly, there are many and they cannot all be discussed here. There is the *control* of content, and the relative responsibilities of governments, regions, institutions, teachers and other interest groups in the planning and accreditation of courses. Curricula at this stage may be more accurately regarded as the outcome of political bargaining than of rational planning. Perceptible shifts in the balance of responsibility and power are occurring in many countries, but not always in the same direction: some are decentralising control while others are centralising. The only general trend is towards the closer involvement of employers in curriculum planning, but even here the form that this takes varies. In countries with a strong tradition of corporate planning involving the "social partners" and formal representation of interest groups, the increased influence of employers flows through the normal channels and tends to affect existing courses. However, where such channels do not exist, or are being bypassed, there is a growth of "customised" courses which lie outside the normal range of provision, and are set up as a result of direct negotiation between employer and provider. Another theme that surfaced in several case-studies was the *modernisation* of content. This was chiefly in relation to technical and vocational education, although it did sometimes refer to information technology or scientific elements in general education. The interest here lies perhaps not so much in what modernisation takes place, as how. There is an obvious need for courses to keep pace with changes in science or technology; but the mechanisms for doing so range from regular consultation leading to evolutionary change, to crash programmes which attempt to revolutionise existing practice.

A different issue is the relationship between content and *gender*, and the pattern of enrolments of young men and women on different types of courses. This is a common concern, reinforced in some countries by projected shortages in certain types of manpower (*sic*) particularly in science and technology. It is difficult to generalise from the studies, but they give the impression that the dissociation between gender and content has gone further in general streams than technical or vocational ones, which still often have strong gender stereotypes, perhaps because of their more direct occupational links. Even in the latter, however, changes are taking place.

Three issues only can be discussed. The first is the concept of "general" education; the second the growing dissociation between the "technical" and "technology"; and the third the development of interpersonal and social skills, particularly in relation to service sector employment.

The emphasis on the need for a solid, basic education for all young people appeared in a number of studies, and was also articulated at the meetings of the authors. The Quebec study pointed to the key role of the lower secondary level as an *école de base*, the emphasis on the "new basics" in the United States has already been mentioned, and current policies for a national curriculum in the United Kingdom appear to be moving in the same direction. The Italian study referred to the importance of a solid educational base several times, not only in terms of knowledge, but cognitive and social skills:

> "The considerations which have governed the launch of these projects relate to the socio-cultural changes of recent years which have made people aware of the necessity of a solid basic education which will allow the individual to develop in an advanced society. The main characteristics of a technical education should involve a range of knowledge which would give confidence and familiarity in science and technology, and an understanding of historical, social and economic processes, enable the individual to live in a constructive and interactive way in the surrounding society, make him capable of using and applying logical processes, and initiate him into the process of personal guidance and apprenticeship. Beyond that, the fundamental objectives of a basic education consist of the capacity to analyse problems, identify solutions, use knowledge in an operational way and acquire new knowledge." (Country study: Italy, p. 13.)

This is in fact written in the context of the development of technical education in Italy, and specifically in relation to experimental curriculum projects which are assisted and recognised by central government. What is striking about the list of aims given above is their broad similarity to those spelled out in some other countries in relation to basic or general education. Does this suggest that Member countries are in fact moving towards the identification of a broadly common core of general education, or do there remain major differences between countries in this respect? Here one encounters again the ambiguities of the term "general" in this field. In Europe, the word general connotes high-level, pre-academic studies, at the top of the pecking order. By contrast, in the United States general streams are lower in the pecking order; in Japan there are variations within the general stream; and to confuse matters further, this report has used the word general to refer not to a type, but a stage of education which precedes the foundation and specific stages.

The issue may be clarified by a conceptual, rather than comparative, analysis. Figure 8 suggests an analytic model of general education. This attempts to answer the questions: basic to what? general in what sense? It identifies three kinds of answers to such questions. An education can be basic/general in terms of *knowledge* (the organised knowledge of disciplines, fields or forms of knowledge); in terms of the *cultural or social system* of which it is a part, which comprises the various sub-systems listed; or in terms of the types of *abilities or potential* which people have and can develop. These three dimensions provide the three main frames of reference for the concept of generality. [The precise headings within each dimension are not important here and are given only as examples[20]].

Like all models, this one is open to question, and theorists can debate, for example, whether one dimension can be reduced to another (is knowledge merely a social construct?) or how far each dimension can be internally differentiated (should we talk of ability or abilities?) However, the model does seem to clarify the various meanings of the word general. It could be argued, for example, that a truly general education, at the lower secondary stage, should be general in terms of all three dimensions: not only should it provide a basis for more advanced studies, but it should equip young people to live as adults in their culture/society, and it should develop them in an all-round way. The scope of general education at this stage will of course reflect the scope of education itself, and responsibilities which in one country will be assigned to the school will in others be the preserve of the family or the task of youth organisations. A *three-dimensional* concept of general education may be difficult to realise in practice, without overloading the curriculum and students, but at a minimum it clarifies in which ways, if any, a curriculum can claim to be general.

At the upper secondary or post-compulsory stage, the model allows one to identify national differences. The traditional pre-academic "general" streams in continental Europe reflect a strong orientation to the *knowledge* dimension, and indeed the headings within those streams are often congruent with the main subject or faculties headings in higher education. By contrast, the concept of general education in the United States reflects both the demands of knowledge and a *socio-cultural* orientation which derives from Dewey and the pragmatists. The balance or tension changes over time, and the current emphasis on "standards" signals a shift back towards organised knowledge as the dominant frame of reference. The United Kingdom pre-academic stream has typically combined specialisation in terms of knowledge, with an espoused commitment to the development of individual *abilities*, in and outside the classroom. General education in Yugoslavia and to a lesser extent Sweden reflects a polytechnical model which reinforces the *social* frame of reference. The academic/general stream in Japan is internally differentiated by curriculum type, with organised knowledge providing the dominant frame of reference in the more "academic" variants, and the "general" variants having a stronger social or developmental emphasis.

All forms of general education involve all three dimensions; it is impossible to conceive of one without the others. All knowledge involves a knower and is situated in a social context; all societies depend on the cognitive representations of their members; and all abilities and skills

Figure 8. **A MODEL OF GENERAL EDUCATION**

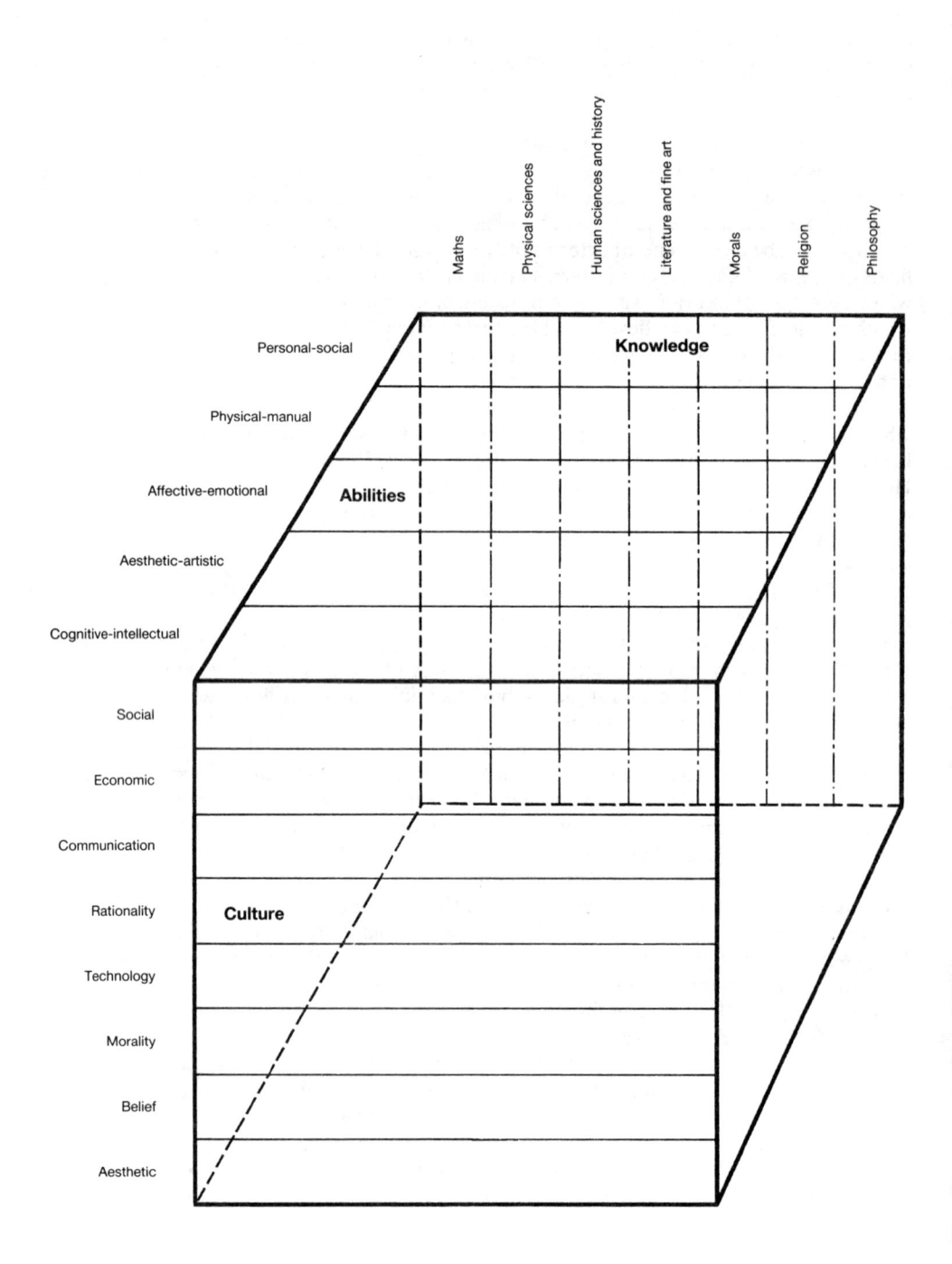

Knowledge axis: Maths, Physical sciences, Human sciences and history, Literature and fine art, Morals, Religion, Philosophy

Abilities axis: Personal-social, Physical-manual, Affective-emotional, Aesthetic-artistic, Cognitive-intellectual

Culture axis: Social, Economic, Communication, Rationality, Technology, Morality, Belief, Aesthetic have a content and context. But there are important differences of emphasis both among and within the three dimensions, and these underlie policy alternatives and policy tensions. In a comparative study, one tends to contrast country with country, but as the German study showed, such tensions can exist within one national (albeit federal) system. The upper stages of the German *Gymnasium* were reformed in 1977/78. The reforms gave students greater, though by no means unrestricted, choice of subjects, and allowed them to specialize if they wished to do so, in contrast to the traditional philosophy of a "broad core". A distinction was made between basic and intensive courses, and there were also changes in assessment and teaching. Since then the reforms have come in for a good deal of criticism, and the main political parties have taken up opposing positions on the issue.

In terms of Figure 8, the debate seems to be between those who adhere to a knowledge-oriented concept of general education, and those who believe that general education should also reflect individual needs and/or social relevance. However, as the study explains, the issue is not quite so straightforward. To begin with, the 1977/78 reforms of the upper secondary curriculum were not accompanied by any change in the entrance requirements for higher education. These give *Abitur* holders general access to virtually any faculty in higher education: a situation which presupposes that upper secondary studies provide a general foundation for all faculties. However, University Rectors now argue that premature specialisation has weakened that foundation; they believe that German, mathematics, two foreign languages, two science subjects and history should be compulsory throughout the upper secondary stage. (Sports, art subjects and religion are also thought to be necessary components of the core curriculum).

The debate also concerns the content and conception of subjects. The view that the curriculum should impart the "classics" challenges the argument that the choice of texts and work should be "derived from the issues and problems that affect pupils' minds and perspectives in our days". There are conflicting views about the very structure and boundaries of subjects, for example the place of history within social studies:

> "Should it maintain its autonomous place or be integrated into a cross-disciplinary, sociologically-oriented course? Since the beginning of the eighties the trend towards 're-stabilizing' the subject of history in the core curriculum has gradually increased in strength. A first landmark in this counter-movement was the decision of the State Supreme Court of Hesse in December 1981. It obliged education authorities to retain German and history as mandatory subjects up to the *Abitur*. This decision, though binding only on the Hessian Ministry of Education, exerted considerable influence on revision-oriented policies all over the Federal Republic." (Country study: Germany, p. 12.)

The argument is thus partly about the structure of disciplines and fields, with the more traditional discipline-based view conflicting with newer problem-oriented, interdisciplinary perspectives. But how traditional is the discipline-based view? The case study argues that the pre-academic model of general education has itself moved away from von Humboldt's original ideal of an "educated citizen". Indeed, it might be more accurate, although certainly more controversial, to see pre-academic general education now as a stage in a long-cycle, high-level vocational education, reflecting the requirements of the academic and other *professions*. (The German professorial model of higher education, which has in fact become the dominant one in modern times, has affinities with the process of apprenticeship, which, given the cultural importance of the latter in Germany, is hardly surprising.) The current situation raises several questions. How far can an aggregation of subject specialisms constitute a "general" education? Is knowledge at this stage better organised in terms of subjects/disciplines or interdisciplinary fields of study? Which "newcomers" to the list of possible studies (e.g. information technology, environmental sciences, health studies) should be added to the core? And can one cover such a wide range of content without resorting to purely didactic or mechanistic teaching methods?

The balance of core and electives in general or pre-academic streams featured in several other case studies. The Japanese study described how the largely "elective" curriculum set up in Japanese comprehensive schools after the war soon gave way to one with a largely prescribed core, partly because of the consequences it would have had for higher education:

> "This system would have been all the more unfavourable for universities, because it would have forced them to establish a host of remedial classes for students entering with different levels of preparation. Clearly, it was more efficient to have upper secondary schools equip students with the necessary foundations upon which they could advance to high-level lectures." (Country study: Japan, p. 28.)

In Japan currently, broadening the scope of students' and schools' choice has become a major policy issue, and the revived attempts to create comprehensive upper secondary schools are attracting widespread attention in this context. But the above historical experience suggests that the success of this or any other attempt to individualise upper secondary studies hinges largely upon how far university entrance requirements and curricula can tolerate them. The balance of core and elective/optional courses is also an issue in the United States, where higher education institutions do in fact provide large numbers of remedial courses (although partly because of a long historical tradition of "access" in some cases). The general point, however, is that it may be more accurate to regard pre-academic courses at the 16-19 stage in many countries not as "general" at all, but as long-cycle foundation courses.

A second major issue in the content of courses is the introduction of technological studies for all or some streams at the post-compulsory stage. This was sometimes subsumed under the general theme of "modernisation" in the case studies, but in other countries it constitutes a major and distinct development. For example, the Technical and Vocational Education Initiative (TVEI) in the United Kingdom:

> "... is focussed on the 14-18 age range of full-time students at schools and colleges and aims to equip those young people to be fully equipped to enter the world of work, to appreciate the practical applications of the qualifications they are attaining, and to develop personal qualities of use to them as employees. This initiative is aimed at an all-ability clientele, and is not simply focussed on the vocational or pre-vocational areas... The emphasis is on learning through doing. The curriculum is outlined in general terms as follows: it should lead towards recognised vocational qualifications; it should not be restricted to one sex; it should contain computer literacy, science and technology, economic awareness, personal and social development; and have some relationship to local factors. TVEI is an all-ability scheme and as such it impinges on the more academic general education. For example its core usually includes English, maths, science, humanities and physical education." (Country study: England and Wales, pp. 14 and 23.)

Two points are worth noting. First, TVEI aims to break the gender-typing which, in the past, has meant that technology was largely a boy's preserve, and it is in fact paralleled by other initiatives aimed at attracting more girls into science and technology in higher education in the United Kingdom, and in other countries. Secondly, the conception of the "technical" here is a broad one; it goes beyond particular subjects or content to embody a general orientation to learning and work.

Comparable developments are taking place in other countries. The Dutch study, for example, notes that from 1988/89, technology will be introduced gradually as part of a new system of basic education for 12-15 year olds. The Curriculum Development Foundation has devised a model curriculum for technology at the lower-secondary stage. In addition, the aims of the NIVO project (New Information Technology in Secondary Schools) are to install fully equipped computer rooms in schools, to provide in-service training for teachers, and to develop "courseware" (software and teaching materials) in schools involved in development projects. Again, one notes that while information technology (IT) plays a key role in such developments, the conception of technology is not restricted to it. There are similar developments in Greece.

In this connection, the Japanese study makes an important distinction between information technology education and information technology training. The former aims to give students a general understanding of computers and their operation and use, while the latter concentrates on programming:

> "... the Science and Vocational Education Council (which is in charge of setting up the main framework of vocational curricula) was cautious not to let upper secondary information education decline into mere computer programme training... In the opinion of this Council, information-processing education should not be pursued by itself but be based on sound technological knowledge about the jobs to which information techniques are applied. This contrasts with the policy of special training schools which aim at the training of computer programmers." (Country study: Japan, p. 64.)

This difference in approach to the promotion of information education can be seen more dramatically in the contrast between the policies of the Ministry of Education and that of the Ministry of International Trade and Industry which proposed a comprehensive plan to introduce computer education into the entire school system (from elementary to upper secondary) on the basis of a projected shortfall of 600 000 software engineers by 1990.

Clearly, there are issues within the development of technology education and IT in particular which deserve more analysis than can be given here. However, the main point that seems to emerge from these and other case studies is that the concept of technology is gradually being widened. In the past, technical education referred to a particular stream which studied particular subjects at a particular level; now technology is acquiring some of the scope and generality that we associate with terms like language, humanities and science. In other words, it is coming to be seen less as a subject and more as a genre of study. Why? One reason may be the shift of emphasis within technology itself, from elements and processes, to control and environment, which was described earlier in this report. It is not that the specific technologies disappear, but that they become subsumed under, and cross-cut by, the newer generic systems technologies. Beyond that, one can only speculate. It may be that we are undergoing one of those long-term shifts in the centre of gravity of our culture which become clear only with hindsight. It is interesting, for example, that some recent work on the relationship between "theory" and "practice" in various fields has come to revalue practice, and see it not simply as the application of theory, but as an activity which has its own characteristics and heuristics; indeed some writers speak of "theories of practice". Such notions are applied not only to the "hard" technologies associated with the natural sciences, but the "softer" behavioural and social technologies, to do with organisation and management, or combinations of the two[21]. The Swedish study referred to the influence of C.P. Snow's[22] notion of the "two cultures" (arts and science) on curriculum planning in the 1960s. But in the 1980s, other dichotomies are emerging, which relate less to the arts/science distinction, than to the pure/applied or natural/artificial one[23]. Concepts such as system, strategy, adaptation, interaction and feedback seem to be gaining a general hold on thinking, and permeating a wide range of fields. Insofar as such concepts are truly generic, they underpin technology's claim to be an essential part of any modern general education, on a par with the established categories of arts and science.

However, the advance of technology into the post-compulsory curriculum still meets some major obstacles. Technology is still widely viewed as the derivation or application of science, so in longer-cycle streams, it tends to be postponed to the post-secondary stage; the argument is that students should concentrate on acquiring a firm scientific foundation at the upper-secondary stage and leave the study of technology until after that. Thus in some countries, technological education has "disappeared up" to tertiary education. But it is a matter of status as well as sequence. As both the United Kingdom studies point out, the impact of technology on the pre-academic streams has so far been relatively limited:

> "There is so far little evidence as to the extent to which TVEI programmes in schools and colleges have actually affected the curriculum undertaken by individual students following A-level courses. In most cases it appears fairly minimal, although new A-level subjects such as Craft, Design and Technology, or Electronic Systems, which have been designed with industrial applications in mind, have appeared. These new A levels do not appear to have the same status, as far as university entrance is required, as the more conventional subjects and hence this reinforces the split in 16-18 work, in schools especially, between the academic stream and the non-academic stream." (Country study: England and Wales, pp. 23-24.)

This status perception may of course change; universities are not wholly above the laws of supply and demand. But it is interesting that the Scottish case study also identifies the problem, although in slightly different terms:

> "The difficulties experienced by TVEI partly reflect teething problems, and we may expect improvement in the future; but the scheme is still likely to be squeezed between two stronger attractions. On the one hand, young people aspiring to higher education may be reluctant to dilute their academic curriculum, and possibly their prospects of qualifying for higher education, by taking TVEI. On the other hand, those seeking employment may find their prospects reduced if they stay in full-time education beyond 16. Not only do many jobs recruit at 16, but YTS schemes (and especially two-year schemes entered at 16) may offer a better chance of subsequent employment." (Country study: Scotland, p. 33.)

This points to the somewhat ambiguous status of TVEI at the present. It could in time acquire a more clearly identified intermediate status, as a middle stream in the system, associated for example with the new City Technology Colleges, and comparable to the full-time technical streams which have existed for many decades in some other European countries.

However, TVEI raises a point of more comparative interest. That is the extent to which both education and employment stages are age-based rather than achievement-based. Despite the variations in student progress, due to repeating and transfers between streams, continental European systems of education and training tend to be relatively age-specific, and the United Kingdom system even more so, although it is worth noting that the Dutch authorities have recently removed the upper age limit of 27 for entrance to apprenticeships. But the major contrast must be with the United States, where as the study notes, "few decisions are irreversible", and the system is extremely flexible in terms of age. Stage theories of education (see Section 2 hereafter) are necessarily age-referenced to some extent, but too rigid an adherence to age limits makes it difficult for the system to accommodate demographic fluctuations. To the extent that courses depend on a cross-sectional demographic intake, they and their staff and institutions are bound to suffer on the demographic roller-coaster.

A related question is the extent to which the labour market in each country is flexible or rigid in terms of age. That question goes well beyond the remit of this report, but it does have consequences for the education and training system. It was noted that in some countries, there has been a shift from "tertiary" to "community" as post-compulsory institutions begin to enrol and seek out larger numbers of adult students. The prime examples here may be the CEGEPs in Quebec and the Community Colleges in the United States. (By contrast, the Swedish upper secondary schools have tended to become more age-specific in recent years, as a consequence of change in admissions policies in those schools and in higher education, and the growth of youth unemployment). But educational flexibility in this respect will mean little unless it is accompanied by flexibility as regards age in the labour market; though no doubt the former has some impact on the latter. This has become an important issue in the recent Japanese reform debate. The Japanese labour market is characterised by rigid age-limits and internal markets:

> "Japanese corporations ... tend to fill vacancies ...not by outside hiring of qualified persons, but by promoting someone from within the organization. Large-scale recruitment of new employees from outside the organization only takes place in April of every year, when new graduates from schools and universities are hired. Under this system, new graduates are assigned to the lowest echelons of the organizations. From there, they are promoted on the basis of skills and knowledge acquired mainly through on-the-job training, until they retire in March of the year when they reach the age of sixty. The massive vacancies brought about by their retirement are filled again by new graduates from schools and universities." (Country study: Japan, p. 53.)

While this pattern has immunised Japan against youth unemployment problems, it is now seen as a source of undue competitiveness and rigidity in the Japanese education system, and the Provisional Council on Educational Reform recently proposed the diversification not only of the criteria for, but timing of, recruitment.

One should not leave the subject of technology without one comment of a more general nature. The rapid growth in power and importance of technological systems carries with it the risk of a certain kind of technological determinism, which sees education as simply responding to the needs "created" by new technology. It is worth remembering that nothing is created by technology itself, only by people. The Yugoslav study cites one statement on this which bears more general repetition:

> "Man does not acquire education to serve technological systems which are objectively given and, in this way, subjugate man by force of his natural necessity, but in order to subjugate technology to himself..." (Country study: Yugoslavia, p. 56.)

The third aspect of content change is the place of personal, interpersonal or social skills in the curriculum. First, it must be recognised that these have always been an element in teaching and learning in all courses, and the fact that they are not, or have not been highlighted as a particular issue does not necessarily mean that they do not exist or are not thought to be important. They are often regarded as being more elusive than some other aspects of the curriculum, and perhaps for that reason have tended to be conceptualised in terms of the teaching process rather than curriculum content. However, they are now becoming an explicit element of content, particularly in some vocational and professional programmes, and were mentioned in passing in several case studies.

This issue picks up again the dimension of "work with people", as distinct from work with information or work with things, introduced in Chapter II, and it relates to the growth of service sector occupations which is clearly indicated by the statistics in Chapter III, although not all such occupations make particular demands on interpersonal or social skills. The idea that education should deliberately develop and assess personal and social skills is, as Cross has pointed out[24], not only unfamiliar, but even repellent to some teachers. It seems to move education too close to socialisation and manipulation for comfort. However, social skills training of various kinds has existed for many years outside the schools, in professional institutes and courses, not least in the management and caring fields, and its importance in other professions, such as medicine, is increasingly being recognised. This training goes under various labels, such as human communications, assertiveness training, leadership, teamwork, counselling and social skills. Besides, relationships with people, whether in the family, workplace or community, are not merely a matter of skills, but of values and awareness. There can be no doubt that pupils in school acquire such skills and awareness anyway, as part of the "hidden curriculum". At a minimum, something might be gained by bringing this more into the open, and analysing what skills and values are being transmitted implicitly in this way. However, any attempt to develop such skills or awareness in a more explicit way depends on identifying those abilities or capacities which underlie work with people in all its diverse forms, and this is difficult. The development of tests of cognitive ability and achievement over many decades has enabled us to identify reasonably accurately the kinds of abilities and skills which enable people to work with information in the most complex sense of that word (i.e. symbol systems and their meanings). Work with information depends on the capacity to conceptualise, abstract, reason and interpret, using what might be called the basic "cognitive codes": natural language, computer language and mathematics. Academic streams in post-compulsory education place a heavy emphasis on the development of such capacities and mastery of such codes. The abilities that underpin work with *things* are less well identified, but can be inferred partly from the methods used to teach such skills. The reliance on demonstration and practice in the teaching of manipulative skills suggests that, for the learner, the abilities to attend, observe and imitate are crucial. Indeed, mimetic abilities may underlie a wide range of skills, from the dramatic to the athletic; anything that involves movement or manipulation requires the capacity to represent and reproduce such skills.

However, it is not easy to identify those abilities or skills which come into play in direct interactions between *people* in a wide range of situations. It may be that the abilities to empathise (to internalise the consciousness of another) and to project (to externalise one's own consciousness) are involved in many such situations. Relating to others implies understanding their "world", and this is central not only in the obvious fields of counselling and care, but in many other kinds of work as well. Likewise, many jobs demand the ability to express, project or communicate one's own ideas and priorities in a way that will engage the attention and interest of others, not only in obvious fields such as sales and marketing, but in all situations where there is some element of leadership or management. Most jobs which involve direct contact with people seem to demand a combination of empathy and projection, sometimes with a varying emphasis (e.g. "soft sell" versus "hard sell" techniques) in sales work. The nurse, for example, has to strike a delicate balance between empathy with, and management of her patients. The whole area of interpersonal and social skills is difficult to analyse, and demands further research. However, its vocational and professional importance seems likely to grow with the growth of service sector occupations, and its general importance in terms of other social relations, in the family and the community, can hardly be doubted.

How then do interpersonal skills fit into the general pattern of education and training for the service sector? As was pointed out earlier, "services" do not constitute a homogeneous educational or training category, but a contrast with traditional craft and manufacturing skills may nevertheless be drawn. Whereas the latter were, and sometimes still are, specific and distinct, the skills needed in services are often multiple and overlapping (see Figure 9). Each kind of service is likely to involve a core skill or skills which are central to the performance of that service, whether it be health, tourism, retailing or clerical work. As the Swedish study noted, such "core skills" are increasingly learned on, and through, the job rather than in educational institutions, though that trend varies from occupation to occupation. However, such core skills need typically to be complemented by other skills which are intrinsic or at least common to services. These include the interpersonal and social skills discussed above; the ability to communicate and relate to colleagues and clients. But they also include organisational skills, not simply in the sense of organising or managing others, but in being a member of a work team, and in self-organisation – planning and prioritising, time-budgeting, self-appraisal, and so on. The latter are particularly important for those who are self-employed. In addition, most people who work in services will need some competence in information skills, both in traditional forms such as filing and modern ones such as data- and word-processing; and some will need financial skills to do with book-keeping, budgeting, handling cash-flow and overheads, and so on. The emphasis on and relationship between these four types of skill and the core skills will of course vary widely from one kind of job to another; but Figure 9 at least exemplifies an alternative training paradigm to the one which historically developed in relation to crafts and manufacturing.

Figure 9.　**TRAINING FOR THE SERVICE SECTOR**

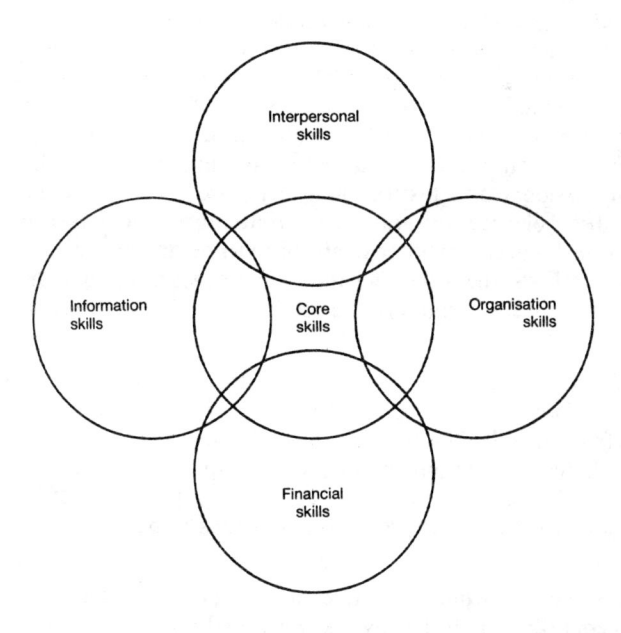

2. The teaching-learning process

Content is always mediated by process: the curriculum is not a paper phenomenon, but is enacted by and through people, materials and environments. Process in this sense refers primarily to the role of the teacher in teaching, the kinds of teaching-learning methods used, the nature of the interaction between students and the environment, both physical and social, in which learning takes place. This is a complex aspect of education, and not the central focus of this report, which is concerned with what is taught rather than how. But in reality the two are inseparable and some comments must, therefore, be made on teaching-learning processes in post-compulsory education. The Yugoslav study, in particular, stressed the importance of what actually goes on in the classroom:

"Many sound ideas presented in programmes and other documents, theoretical papers and so on, are sometimes realised in a less successful way... For example, the emphasis on higher cognitive and non-cognitive aspects of instruction, which can often be found in them (sometimes with a criticism of exaggerated demands on students' factual knowledge) is not always followed in teaching practice. In the everyday classroom routine the emphasis is often on the knowledge of mere facts. The stress on higher cognitive aims, the ability to use knowledge, finding needed facts, the affective aims, and so on, are sometimes present, but never to a satisfactory degree... In the real classroom setting, because of overloaded programmes, a very small part of teachers' time and strength usually remains for engagements with the 'higher aims'. A lack of extrinsic motivation of teachers (neither financial nor moral) is another cause of this situation." (Country study: Yugoslavia, pp. 32 and 34.)

The study goes on to note that changes in educational practice are always relatively slower than in educational organisation.

The general implication of such comments is that *curriculum* development cannot be dissociated from both *staff* development and *organisation* development. Because of the highly contingent nature of the teaching-learning process (the answer to many pedagogical questions is "it depends") teachers have, and have to have, considerable "discretion" in the way they work, even in tightly planned courses. Curricula are therefore always interpreted rather than simply delivered. Moreover, the teaching-learning process is inextricably bound up with organisational features, from the mundane issues of timetabling up through the complex questions about professional and institutional structures. The curriculum thus goes well beyond the specification of programmes or the production of educational materials.

The comments in this section will be confined to three main "process" issues: changes in teaching styles and methods; the workplace as a learning environment; and the phenomenon of the "working student". The Scottish case study notes that changes in teaching may be related to changes in students:

"...The second and related shift is in the composition of the student body, which now includes many more young people with few or no qualifications from compulsory schooling and from unskilled family backgrounds. Many of these 'new' students are from backgrounds where post-compulsory education and training would not normally have been contemplated; this, together with their frequently poor job prospects, results in problems of motivation and has provided a stimulus to pedagogical reform." (Country study: Scotland, p. 19.)

The stimulus for reform is not wholly negative, however; it seems that there is a search in the United Kingdom generally, partly led by the Further Education Unit, for what might be described as a "new pedagogy" which is more appropriate to the needs of late adolescents and young adults:

> "Add to this (student-centredness) the processes central to the delivery of a curriculum to which a student can feel a sense of personal involvement and ownership, as detailed in *Vocational Preparation* (FEU:1981), of negotiation, counselling, guidance and assessment, and there begins to be acknowledged a movement emphasizing the centrality of the student to the process of learning rather than the centrality of the content of that which is learned. This represents a major shift of emphasis, the consequences of which have yet to reverberate fully around the rest of the education system." (Country study: England and Wales, p. 17.)

Likewise, the Scottish study identifies an emerging concept of education which

> "...while far from consensual, is implied in most current developments. It embraces such themes as relevance, activity-based and student-centred learning, problem-solving, learning to learn, personal effectiveness and personal and social development. The concept is organised primarily around pedagogy and methods of assessment, and the belief that reforming these will enable more generic skills and competencies to be better developed. Since this approach is not defined in terms of content it is applied to a wide variety of curricula, both academic and technical/vocational, and to all sectors of education and training." (Country study: Scotland, p. 28.)

But do such changes affect all streams equally? Elsewhere, the Scottish study contrasts the student-centred approaches of some newer developments with the more traditional teacher-centred approach of many first-year higher education courses. In other studies, the implicit contrast is between student-centred and subject-centred, especially where the latter is dominated by examinations. Heavily loaded subject-centred curricula impose didactic teaching methods, and can lead to a superficial, "encyclopaedic" approach to learning. This problem seems to occur mainly in traditional pre-academic streams, and was mentioned in the German, Swiss and Japanese studies: indeed the latter are commonly referred to as an "examination hell" and current policies are designed to mitigate their effects, partly by reducing the required number of credits and hours. By contrast, some U.S. institutions are increasing both credit requirements and "time on task" in a renewed emphasis on quality and standards. Several case studies also noted the increased use of continuous assessment, partly to modify the effects of formal examinations on curricula and teaching. But several of the studies leave the general impression that innovations in teaching and assessment are more likely to occur in the lower-status or marginal programmes or courses, than in the well-established high-status pre-academic streams. This may be unsurprising but it does mean that such innovations may become tainted by association, and hence fail to become more widely adopted.

Despite the problems of innovating in teaching, several studies stressed the importance of teacher training, both pre-service and in-service, for maintaining standards and developing provision. As the Swiss study notes, both the authorities and the public there are very well aware of the fact that the quality of education depends in large part on the competence of the educators. "From this comes the need to give the latter as deep and up-to-date an initial preparation as possible, as well as systematic continuing education." On a different issue, the Dutch study reports that the government there intends to make more use of the teaching expertise available within industry by recognising practical experience as an adequate qualification for teaching on some technical courses, and introducing flexible rules concerning appointments and in-service training.

The second aspect of process which was mentioned above was the use of the workplace as an environment for learning. The extent to which this happens depends on whether the pattern of vocational education in a given country follows the "schooling" or "dual" model. The Swiss study presents the classic argument for the latter:

"...many young people are saturated by the full-time studies they have followed to the age of 15/16 and want the more adult mode of training which apprenticeship to an employer is. We must therefore concentrate on remotivating this type of young people so that they get an appetite for the work that apprenticeship to their trade involves, as well as the indispensable studies which go with it. And if these initial objectives are reached, then we must search for ways to move on to new ones, such as the wish to deepen and complete, through more theoretical studies, the general training they have acquired." (Country study: Switzerland, p. 5.)

The emphasis on the workplace as an environment for learning at the post-compulsory stage is not, however, confined to those countries which have strong apprenticeship systems. Indeed as opportunities for apprentices in the United Kingdom have declined, mainly because of the decline of the traditional manufacturing industries with which they were associated, the emphasis on "work-driven" learning, to use the Manpower Services Commission's phrase, has grown:

"As the opportunity for jobs has declined for the age group, so the interest in the workplace as a centre for learning has increased. This in part is due to the inclination of young people to regard it as having a greater potential for employment. But there is plenty of evidence to indicate that work experience is valued by young people; it is invariably ranked as one of the most interesting components of pre-vocational schemes. There is little doubt that people learn best when they achieve a sense of purpose from what they are doing. The workplace, as long as such a term is considered in its widest possible context, provides the opportunity for such a sense of purpose. Hence the interest in YTS, which is based mainly in the workplace, and in CPVE and TVEI, where work experience (simulated or real) and work shadowing, are encouraged." (Country study: England and Wales, p. 38.)

Clearly such work experience has to be planned and stimulating rather than routine or haphazard to be useful, and it is always more difficult to regulate the practical side of vocational education than the educational side. Considerable variations in the quality of work experience may be expected, some of them due to the limitations of small companies or difficult economic situations, and others due to the lack of training or aptitude among the trainers or supervisors. It is worth noting that countries with well-established apprenticeship systems, such as Germany and Switzerland, also have well-established systems for training on-the-job trainers; indeed their role may be as pivotal in a "dual" system, not only cognitively but affectively, as the role of the classroom teacher is in a "schooling" one. In this context, it is interesting to note the current attempts in the United Kingdom to develop the role of the "industrial tutor" in a comparable way. Whatever the problems of work-based training, however, the current emphasis on the workplace as a learning environment provides an interesting challenge to the "environmental monopoly" of education institutions, and if nothing else, forces them to demonstrate that what they do cannot be done, or done as well, elsewhere.

It is interesting to speculate also what effect the current emphasis on the workplace as an environment for initial vocational training at the post-compulsory stage will have on employers' and policy-makers' perception of continuing vocational education. There may be danger that the current emphasis on continuing education and training for those in employment will be interpreted in purely formal or overt terms; continuing education could be seen largely as a matter of *courses*, either in-house or external. This may be partly because such courses allow organisers to be seen to be doing something, and fit neatly into standard bureaucratic procedures. But both adult learning theory, and practice in some countries such as Japan, suggest that non-formal continuing education is at least as important as formal courses, if not more[25]. In this perspective, training becomes a normal part of all supervisory and managerial jobs, and takes place mainly in and through the normal processes of work and innovation, as for example in the Japanese "quality circles". Such practices reinforce the concept of the workplace as a learning environment, and the organisation as a *learning culture*.

It is a short step from the above to the issue of the accreditation of learning that is entirely work-based, or purely "experiential". This has been a significant development in the United States in the last decade, and has made some headway in the United Kingdom. It was referred to in the Scottish case study, in relation to work-based modules. However, since it is an issue which relates mainly to higher and continuing adult education, which has been discussed in a recent OECD report[26], it will be left aside here. Students at the post-compulsory stage typically have not yet accumulated enough experience either in work or outside to be considered for accreditation, and such experience as they do gain is often already within a formally accredited training framework. However, this is not to say that they may not be allowed some credit on an informal and case-by-case basis for their existing work experience when enrolling in some courses.

Finally, under the heading of process, one must mention the phenomenon of the "working student". The work that such students do is not, as above, part of their planned education or training; it is for their own benefit. The working student has long been associated with the United States: as the United States study points out, "A large fraction of high school students hold jobs. Policy-makers have generally applauded this behaviour. The work behaviour of high school students appears to be a uniquely American phenomenon". In fact it is not, although it is more common in the United States than elsewhere. But the Quebec study notes:

> "This phenomenon is becoming as widespread as in the United States. Studies of it are in progress in several colleges. It is difficult to summarize them, because they used different means of collecting data. However, one constant has already emerged: the majority of those who work do 15 or more hours per week, in restaurant or sales work, and for pocket money not economic survival." (Country study: Quebec, Canada, p. 34.)

There is evidence of substantial student working in some European countries too, for example in France, and Italy. However, since labour regulations in some European countries forbid such work on pain of withdrawal of student support or status (which may carry important financial concessions in travel and other areas) the statistics are unreliable, and form part of the "grey" economy. But because enrolment fees are low in some countries, it makes economic sense, even if it is not economically imperative, for some students to spin out their studies over a period of years while they work part-time. Such students are technically full-time, but in fact part-time or intermittent, and this fact helps to explain the discrepancy between formal course length and actual completion times.

As to the details and effects of student working, the United States study cites some interesting research. White students work more than non-white students; higher achievers are somewhat less likely to work than low achievers; those whose parents have high incomes are somewhat more likely to work. As to the consequences for educational achievement and future employment, the picture is less clear. In no studies has working been shown to have a positive effect on the student's grade point average; but negative effects may be limited to those who work a lot – say more than 15 or 20 hours per week. The extent to which outside work interferes with studies depends also on the amount of homework (study) that has to be done, and the average high-school student spends less than an hour per day on homework. College students who work earn more when they graduate, and are more likely to graduate.

The case study discusses the research evidence on student working at more length than is possible here, and the reader is referred to it for further detail. Unfortunately, there are not comparable data from other studies which would allow comparisons to be made. It could be that the pattern of student working reflects differing educational structures and labour market conditions in different countries. Part of the research problem lies in picking up the less measurable effects of such work on attitudes, employability and socialisation, which may again vary from country to country. A lot depends on how educators, employers and others view such activity, and whether it is considered "normal" or not. Two general points can be made. First, it is worth remembering that full-time education is a relatively recent phenomenon in historical terms. Even systems which were formally full-time earlier in this century or before were effectively part-time for many students, as the high truancy rates show. In country schools, children were often taken away at harvest time by their parents to help on the land, and in urban areas, educators and administrators had to fight a long battle to protect children from the demands of urban labour in factories, shops and elsewhere; (a situation which exists in many developing countries today). Much further and higher education was effectively part-time, with students working during the day and attending classes in the evening. Current economic and employment trends may or may not reinforce the trend towards student working. On the one hand, formal policies are geared mainly to delaying entry to the labour market, partly in order to reduce youth unemployment, and partly to upgrade the workforce. On the other hand, part-time and casual jobs are growing faster than full-time ones in some economies, and some government policies are aimed at deregulating the labour market. The latter trends might make part-time work more attractive for students, especially if they coincide with a decline in direct financial support for studying. And modular course structures, which are discussed below, make it easier for students to pursue a more intermittent pattern of studies. The whole question illustrates yet another way in which the education market and labour market interact at the post-compulsory stage.

3. The structure of courses

The third and final aspect of the curriculum is its structure. The structure of courses provides the framework within which content and process exist. Structure constitutes the format of knowledge; and because the pattern of assessment and certification typically maps onto the structure of the courses, structure serves to relate one course to another, and to the labour market. Course structures raise some complex questions, which can only be touched on here, but it may be useful initially to see such structures in terms of a continuum going from the purely linear to the purely modular, as below:

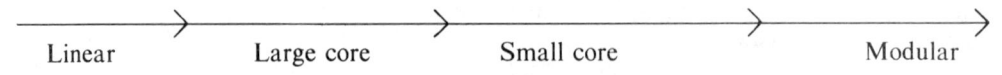

| Linear | Large core | Small core | Modular |

In linear courses, the student follows a defined line of study which has a pre-determined sequence; no divergence from this is possible. As one moves along the continuum the structure becomes less and less linear, and the student has more and more options. Many courses have a large core or "trunk" which may occupy two-thirds or three-quarters of the student's time; the remaining fraction, often towards the end of the course, is left open to choice. The core may however be smaller than that, constituting only a half or one-third of the total; and when the core falls below that proportion, people tend to begin talking of "modularity". A purely modular course would simply be a set of "building-blocks", with no predetermined sequence at all. Because the blocks have to be interchangeable in terms of timetabling and assessment weighting, they tend to become standardised in length and size, although it is possible to work out a standard weighting system for non-standard blocks, sometimes referred to as a tariff system, and to distinguish between different levels of module. In practice, purely linear and purely modular structures are quite rare, since most courses allow for some element of choice, even if only within components, and few courses can afford to dispense entirely with linear requirements and sequence. In practice also, the ideal curriculum is usually modified by constraints of timetabling, staffing and resources. Many courses which are referred to as "lines of study" or "modular systems" in fact lie somewhere between the two ends of the continuum[27].

Considerable variations in course structures are, however possible, and this fact emerged from the case studies. It is difficult to generalise, because the structures vary not only from country to country, but from stream to stream and even course to course within a country. However, bearing in mind this caveat, one can say that the dominant form of course structure in most of continental Europe is linear. The term "line of study" applies to the majority of courses in Germany, Switzerland, France and Italy. It is also the standard term in Sweden, but there current policies suggest a shift towards a more modular pattern. The Netherlands also seem to be moving away from a linear to a more modular pattern. The Yugoslav system contains both lines of study, and 2+2 general plus vocational patterns, depending on the region. England and Wales, like Sweden, seem to be moving gradually in a modular direction, but Scotland has already modularised about two-thirds of all post-compulsory provision. The Japanese system seems predominantly linear, with little mention of modularity except for marginal groups. In the United States (where the term module is used in a slightly different sense to refer to discrete learning packages) the basic structure of the curriculum has been modular (in this sense) for decades. Students earn qualifications by building up course credits which are usually transferable. There may be restrictions on choice, in the form of inbuilt sequences or distribution requirements, but compared to the European or Japanese systems, "electives" play a large part in the curriculum; indeed, there are pressures in the United States to reaffirm the importance of core requirements, and reduce the proportion of options. In the CEGEPs in Quebec, the organisation of courses "obeys the principles of modularity and combination, which allow various combinations with a limited number of elements. All the professional and pre-university programmes have the same structure". Clearly, the structure of the post-compulsory curriculum varies from country to country, although it must again be stressed that these generalisations do not necessarily apply to all streams or courses; also, as was pointed out above, few courses are wholly linear or wholly modular. Rather than engaging in straightforward international comparisons therefore, it may be more useful to examine the rationale behind each kind of structure.

What are the advantages of structuring the curriculum in "lines of study"? From the references made earlier to the labour market, it will be clear that lines of study corresponded in the past, and to some extent still correspond, to the structure of labour. Jobs were, and often still are, specific, well-defined and relatively stable in content and process. They were, and often still are, clearly demarcated horizontally from other jobs, and stratified vertically in terms of the level of job. In such circumstances, the most rational way to structure post-compulsory education is to identify distinct lines and levels of study which correspond to the structures of employment: a plumbing line prepares people to be plumbers, a pharmacy or catering line to be pharmacists or caterers. A linear structure like this does not prevent changes taking place within the line; far from it. The very fact that the line is clearly defined means that it is relatively easy to see what kinds of changes might be needed: there is an unambiguous point of reference. Adjunct skills can be included or "bought in" if necessary. There is nothing to prevent such lines including some element of choice within them, particularly at the later stages, in order to accommodate individual differences or labour market diversity (for example, between working for small or large firms). And lines of study can serve to standardise or "harmonise" courses in different regions or parts of a country.

Over and above these labour market arguments, however, there are pedagogical and psychological reasons for organising studies in lines. Lines of study ensure continuity; teachers can take it for granted that B will have been preceded by A; and if A has not been well taught, the effects will soon become clear, and something can be done. Lines of study also ensure interaction: they bring together, and keep together, students for a substantial period of time, which means that they can support and learn from one another. They allow permanent relationships to be built up between students and staff, and provide role models to imitate or react against. They offer the student a clear identity and sense of belonging at a time in his or her life when the development of identity is important. Lines of study help to bridge the transitions of early adulthood.

These are powerful arguments, and it is little wonder that this pattern of study is so well established in so many countries. Indeed the criticisms of the distinct and self-contained line of study often bear not on the principle, but on the way it is put into practice. There is sometimes an in-built conservatism in such lines which fails to keep up with the times; teachers get out of touch both with their own field of practice, and with what is happening in other courses. The monopoly of provision sometimes leads to complacency. New knowledge and requirements are continually added to courses, but nothing is taken away. The teacher can become remote or dictatorial, the group claustrophobic or conflict-ridden, the identity restrictive rather than reassuring. There is little room for creative uncertainty; little relativity of perspective. The whole experience can degrade into something mechanical and superficial.

Such shortcomings can no doubt be remedied by teacher training, especially in-service training, regular course evaluation, better links with the external world, and other fairly obvious measures. However, the shift away from lines of study as a way of organising the curriculum is for more fundamental reasons, reasons which are spelled out in several of the case studies. For example, the Dutch study, commenting on the development of modular structures in technical courses, stresses their potential for innovation:

"Arranging the subject matter in modules will allow the structure and content of technical courses to be adapted more rapidly to changes in the qualifications required without having to 'reshuffle' the entire curriculum, as has been the case up to now, due to rigid subject divisions. Specific modules can be adapted after consultation between schools and industry, without close government intervention; the internal assessment and examination of students per module can be tailored to the wishes of local employers, within government standards." (Country study: Netherlands, p. 18.)

As noted earlier, the Swedish study argues that modularity is a reflection of changes in the actual structure of work. In France, modular courses in vocational education are used to meet the specific problems of particular groups: young people lacking in motivation, adults who require greater flexibility. The United States study describes the flexibility that the transferability of credits gives students and the system:

> "A notable feature of post-secondary education in the United States is the transferability of credits to different programs and schools. A longitudinal survey of the 1980 high school seniors who enrolled in higher education after graduation reveals that about 14.2 per cent of the public 2-year college students transferred to other schools in the first year and 31.4 per cent transferred in the second year. Among the latter, 77.8 per cent transferred to 4-year colleges. In other words, approximately a quarter of 2-year college graduates did not quit schooling but advanced to 4-year colleges and universities. Another study also indicated that over 60 per cent of those in the high school class of 1972 who received bachelor's degrees by 1984 had attended two or more institutions, and that 11 per cent had earned Associate's degrees from 2-year colleges en route to their bachelor's degrees." (Country study: United States, p. 27.)

Credit transfer not only allows students to move from one institution and course to another, but to move in and out of the system. The United States study cites longitudinal research which monitored the pattern of enrolment/non-enrolment of high school seniors over a five-year period. Using a binary code to indicate enrolled/non-enrolled status, they identified thirty-two different patterns. e.g. 10101, 11011, 11101. The research found that among those who had ever enrolled, 22.6 per cent interrupted their studies and moved in and out of formal schooling.

Modularity (in this definition) is however the norm in the United States, and perhaps one would not expect a very detailed analysis of it from there. Indeed the United States study was more concerned with the trends towards reinforcing *core* requirements in upper-secondary and post-secondary curricula, as implied by terms such as "basics", "excellence" and "quality": a shift perhaps towards the other end of the continuum. (It is interesting to note, in passing, the role of foreign comparisons in policy debates; whereas current debate in the United Kingdom often refers to Germany, especially in the vocational field, and European systems are to some extent compared with one another and with North America, in the United States the main point of reference now seems to be Japan. All such comparisons are selective, and the choice of country reveals something about current national priorities and concerns.)

Not surprisingly however, the most detailed discussion of modularity was with reference to the country which has moved most recently and most sharply in that direction: Scotland. There is not space in this report to convey that analysis in its full depth, and only a few aspects will be treated here. The case study first describes the new structure, which currently covers (in OECD terms) technical and vocational streams but not general ones:

> "... nearly all non-advanced vocational courses for post-compulsory students in Scotland have been replaced by a system of modules, usually of a notional 40 hours' duration, accredited by a single National Certificate. Modules may be taken at college or school or, for a small but increasing proportion, at centres outside the formal education system; students may study modules offered in more than one institution; credits are transferable. Courses are therefore replaced by programmes of modules; the certificate records the individual modules completed by a student and does not give them any group title, although as a transitional measure systems of equivalences have been published which relate modules to pre-existing group certificates and to other United Kingdom qualifications, and certificates may be endorsed with these equivalences. Each module is specified through a centrally validated module descriptor the most important element of which is a list of learning outcomes; the Action Plan provided an opportunity to revise and update the curriculum, cutting out unnecessary content and increasing the emphasis on competencies." (Country study: Scotland, pp. 6 and 8.)

The case study goes on to describe the reasons for the introduction of the new structure:

"The rationale for the modular system concerns, first, the efficient use of resources. Common elements of different group certificate courses are replaced by single modules; duplication between courses and between institutions is reduced. Second, the system is designed to enhance choice and flexibility. Programmes may be assembled flexibly from the 2 000 modules currently available; students changing their career plans, or undergoing retraining, receive credit for relevant modules already covered; the principle of credit transfer is thus extended. There is flexibility in pacing; learning may be extended over differing periods of time. The system has multiple entry and exit points: a student entering further education is not committed to completing a full course in order to receive credit; conversely, students have an incentive to build on modules they have picked up at school or on YTS [Youth Training Scheme]. These points illustrate a third theme, that the modular system is intended to increase participation. Fourth, the modules provide a convenient 'curricular currency' for planning the curriculum, especially in negotiation between colleges and employers or YTS managing agents. Finally, and relatedly, the modules provide a flexible framework that can accommodate further innovations in education and training, for example the need for relevant and certificated inputs to YTS and TVEI and the developments in work-based learning." (Country study: Scotland, p. 8.)

The Scottish study examines various aspects of the new modular structure, several of which can be mentioned here. First, as already mentioned, the system covers the "technical" and "vocational" streams but not the "general" one. Why not? The original plan did hint that the general stream ("Highers") might eventually be included within it, but neither that, nor the separate modularisation of Highers is currently likely. This has not however prevented some schools from offering both modular and non-modular (i.e. pre-academic) options, often on the basis of consortia with other schools and colleges, and some students on general streams are now "topping up" their pre-academic studies with the odd vocational module. It is worth noting that the pattern of innovation is similar in the Netherlands: modules have been introduced first into technical/vocational education, and their incursion into general streams, although planned, has yet to come.

Two points suggest themselves. First, the "resistance" of general streams to modularity may be a matter of status, or it may reflect the essentially preparatory, rather than specific, function which such courses perform. The analysis in Chapter II suggested that different streams may be at different stages at the same age; a sixteen-year-old on a pre-academic course may still be at the general stage whereas a comparable student on a technical course may be at the foundation stage, and one on a short-cycle vocational course already be at the specific stage. In reality the stages are not quite as clear-cut as this, but the notion of stages suggests one reason why the acceptability of modularity might decrease with the level of studies: the concepts of generality and foundation preclude or limit the notion of choice. The other point that emerges concerns the relationship between institutions and curricula in educational policy. Much of the description of, and debate about, post-compulsory education, is couched in terms of *institutions*. Should they be comprehensive or differentiated? Should they be colleges or schools? How far should education take place outside educational institutions altogether, for example in the workplace? What the Scottish study suggests is that the introduction of a modular curriculum structure to some extent undercuts this institutional debate. For the student, the essential element becomes the *curriculum module*, not the institution, and he or she can use credit transfer to move between institutions. That shift of focus, from institutions to curricula and qualifications, is potentially important for policy.

A second major issue has to do with how modules are validated and controlled, and here the Scottish study distinguishes between input and output controls.

"In the strong version of the output model, controls would be exercised through outputs only; modules would be specified only by the learning outcomes and the related performance criteria; where, when and how the student studied for modules would be at the discretion of the student and/or teacher; there would be no direct regulation or control of inputs." (Country study: Scotland, p. 39.)

However, adequate output control is difficult to achieve. Assessment can only sample learning, and assessment measures are themselves sometimes invalid or unreliable. Modules are often assessed by those who provide them, rather than centrally, and this can lead to variations in standards. Learning outcomes in any case do not include the hidden curriculum and the unintended but possibly important side-effects of teaching. So, in practice, output measures are supplemented by input measures: where was the module studied? who taught it? what facilities were available? what kind of institution was it? Such considerations tend to modify the principle of credit transfer, and as the study noted, institutions may sometimes require a student to repeat a module that he or she has studied elsewhere, in the belief that it was not properly covered, or that adequate equipment was not available. Thus the success of the system depends heavily on the perceived validity of its output measures:

"Assessment may prove to be the stress point of the modular system, and also of YTS. The credibility of assessment and certification is central to the modular reform. It is critical for progression: if modules do not have credit students will come to be judged on the basis of where, when or in what status they took the modules, or of their previous attainments in compulsory education. The problem becomes more serious as restrictions on access to modules are relaxed; it becomes particularly acute with the projected use of modules to accredit work-based and even experiential learning." (Country study: Scotland, p. 38.)

The final issue raised by the Scottish study relates to the concept of an "education market" broached in Chapter II of this report. The study suggests that there are, not one, but two kinds of market. There is a pre-employment market in which the immediate consumers are the students themselves. However, students' pre-employment choices anticipate the future demands on them of employers and higher education. These demands tend to reinforce "academic" values; not only higher education institutions, but many employers tend to prize potential rather than competence, general ability rather than specific skills. By contrast, in the in-employment market, the employers are the direct consumers. They are interested now in courses which promise direct relevance and immediate competence, rather than general preparation or development. The function of certification is different in the two markets. In the pre-employment market, it is primarily used as a means of screening or selecting possible employees, not only in terms of ability and potential, but with an eye to attitudes and socialisation as well. In the in-employment market, employers use certification mainly as an accounting device and a guarantee that they are getting what they have paid for. Both markets have distortions, and one can identify segmented markets within each. So the whole concept of an education market itself becomes much more complex.

The modular system attempts to serve these two rather dissimilar education markets, with different degrees of success. The system has difficulties in relation to the pre-employment market, not only because universities are reluctant to recognise the modules, but because the absence of levels or grades means that they cannot be used to differentiate students in the normal educational way: they are criterion-referenced in a sector of the system which in fact requires norm-referencing. By contrast, the system appears to work well in the in-employment education market, because it provides an overt and yet flexible basis for planning and negotiating in-service education and training with employers and employees.

However, it is not just a question of trying to serve two masters; the policy emphasis has itself shifted since the system was first mooted, from the pre-employment market to the in-employment one.

"Initially, much of the rhetoric emphasized the increased choice, flexibility and opportunities for progression that the modular system offered the individual student. It identified the reform with an extension of comprehensive education and appeared to point towards the sociological concept of 'contest' mobility, in which educational selection decisions are postponed and a chance of mobility remains open for longer. This rhetoric is consonant with the perspective of the pre-employment market. More recently a different emphasis has predominated: flexibility and progression are still key themes but they are related to the training needs of employers and the demands of work and of labour markets (internal as well as external). The switch in rhetorical style may partly reflect current preoccupations, notably with work-based learning, but it may also reflect the greater success of modules in relation to the in-service market." (Country study: Scotland, p. 43.)

This shift in policy emphasis and style has occurred more generally over the last two decades, not only in Scotland but in many OECD countries.

4. Final remarks

The main policy issues which arise out of this study are summarised at the beginning of the report, and no attempt will therefore be made here to draw any general conclusions. As the Secretariat's summary points out, the aim of the report is as much to clarify the questions and issues, as to suggest solutions. The analysis in the body of the report will hopefully have served to warn of the dangers of simplistic generalisation. It may be useful finally, however, to indicate some of the aspects of post-compulsory education which the report was not able to explore, because of limitations of time or data, but which seem nevertheless to be important.

One aspect of post-compulsory education which causes concern is that of wastage rates, through drop-out or failure. This was addressed in several studies, in particular the United States one, and was voiced at the meetings of authors. Unfortunately, the comparative data which would have allowed a more thorough discussion of the problem could not be gathered in the time available. However, the issue does point up the distinction between *formal access* and *real accessibility* to education. Systems having in many cases established the first may now need to move to monitor the second, in terms of the extent to which students and institutions really are adapted to one another; otherwise the open door may prove to be a revolving door.

A second obvious issue is that of guidance and counselling, which was the subject of comment in many studies, and in particular the Swiss and the United Kingdom ones. Because this stage of education concentrates educational choice and selection more than any other, the role of information and guidance is more central than at any other stage. Two points can be made. First, because choice and selection are so integral to post-compulsory education, there is an argument (voiced in the England/Wales case study) for training most "front-line" teachers, trainers and supervisors to some depth in this aspect of their work, partly because students may find it easier to discuss such problems and choices with people with whom they already have a teaching-learning relationship, than with someone whom they have never met before. But the complexity of the system and of students' choices also point to the need for a professional and systemic service, which ranges well beyond the "local knowledge" that teachers typically have.

This last point raises another issue, to do with the local or regional dimension of post-compulsory education, an aspect which was discussed in several case studies, in particular the Swedish and Yugoslav ones. This may be important for several reasons. First, many young adults, particularly from vocational streams, are recruited into local labour markets rather than national ones, and their recruitment may depend less on formal qualifications than on the kind of "employability" that comes from contact – either direct or indirect – with an employer. Secondly, the report has suggested that local networks, consortia or federations of providers may become more common in the future. And thirdly, rapid economic change, and especially the decline of traditional manufacturing industries can lead quite rapidly to the kinds of regional imbalances which were previously associated only with industrialisation rather than de-industrialisation. Such factors point to the importance of regional analyses of post-compulsory education.

The relationship between initial, post-compulsory education, and continuing education for adults also raises questions which may become increasingly important in the future. The model presented in this report implies that continuing adult education belongs mainly to the "specific" or subsequent "open" stages of the educational cycle, but in reality the pattern may be less linear, and some adults will need not simply to update or refine their skills, but to lay a completely new foundation for their work. Should such provision be made alongside or separately from that for 16-19 year-olds? How different should the approaches and methods for adults be? What are the advantages and disadvantages of age segregation? What policies are Member countries pursuing in this regard? The importance of such questions will in some countries be increased by a demographic pattern which shifts the emphasis towards older cohorts in the next decade.

One final point may be made. Purely structural comparisons of education systems, which focus on the pattern of institutions, qualifications and courses, may be of limited use because some of the most important effects of education are less visible. The importance of this aspect of education has been suggested by both educationists and economists. Educationists have pointed out that the formal curriculum is only part of what is taught, and have explored what has come to be labelled the "hidden curriculum" of courses and institutions: those implicit messages which are embodied and transmitted in what is taught and how and where it is taught. Economists likewise have pointed out that formal labour contracts are inherently incomplete, and that workers always have a hidden element of "discretion" in how they work. Such discretion is influenced by individual attitudes and group norms. This points to the potential importance of such cultural variables in economic performance, though the nature and impact of these remains rather speculative.

One of the reasons why post-compulsory education is a complex field of policy is that it brings together the two broad policy themes which have dominated the last two decades: education and equality, and education and the economy. Both these presuppose a relatively direct relationship between education and society. Both themes remain central to any analysis of the post-compulsory field, and both have run like *leitmotivs* through this report. But it may be that some of the most important effects of post-compulsory education are indirect rather than direct, influencing the cultural variables which in turn affect both social relations and economic performance.

NOTES AND REFERENCES

1. LAUGLO, J. (1983) "Concepts of 'general education' and 'vocational education' curricula for post-compulsory schooling in western industrialised countries: when shall the twain meet?", *Comparative Education*, 19(3), 285-304; and SQUIRES, G. (1987) *The Curriculum Beyond School*, Hodder and Stoughton, London, pp. 26-50.
2. See Chapter III, Table 1.
3. United States Department of Labor (1965) *Dictionary of Occupational Titles* (3rd edition), United States Government Printing Office, Washington, D.C.
4. OECD, "The Evolution of New Technology, Work and Skills in the Service Sector", OECD/CERI, Paris, 1986; "New Technology and Human Resource Development in the Automobile Industry", OECD/CERI, Paris, 1986.
5. OECD (1983) *Policies for Higher Education in the 1980s*, OECD, Paris, Part Two, Chapter III.
6. This kind of argument derives partly from HAYEK, F. (1944) *The Road to Serfdom*, George Routledge, London.
7. This has been dealt with in the CERI Project on "Changing Work Patterns and the Role of Education and Training" in 1986.
8. OECD (1973) *Short-Cycle Higher Education: a search for identity*, Paris; and OECD (1987) *Universities Under Scrutiny*, Paris.
9. OECD (1977) *Selection and Certification in Education and Employment*, Paris.
10. National Commission on Excellence in Education (1984), *A Nation at Risk: the imperative for educational reform*. U.S. Government Printing Office, Washington, D.C.
11. WIENER, M. (1981) *English Culture and the Decline of the Industrial Spirit*, Cambridge University Press, Cambridge.
12. BERTRAND, O. and MARECHAL, P. (1981) *The Classification of Skilled Workers in the Member States of the European Community*, CEDEFOP, Berlin.
13. EURICH, N.P. (1985) *Corporate Classrooms: The Learning Business*, Princeton University Press, Princeton, N.J.
14. COUNCIL OF EUROPE (1979) *Occupational Basic Training*, Council for Cultural Co-operation, Strasbourg.
15. PERRY, W.G. (1970) *Forms of Intellectual and Ethical Development in the College Years*, Holt, Rinehart and Winston, New York.
16. GRIGNON, C. (1971) *L'ordre des choses*, Minuit, Paris; GLEESON, D. (ed.) (1983) *Youth Training and the Search for Work*, Routledge and Kegan Paul, London; and WATSON, K. (ed.) (1983), *Youth, Education and Employment – International Perspectives*, Croom Helm, London.
17. This aspect of the training or preparation of post-compulsory teachers was implicit in several of the case studies which laid emphasis on the pivotal role of the teacher or supervisor at this stage; see in particular the Quebec, United Kingdom, Swiss and Yugoslav studies.

18. The concept of "level" is illuminated by the analysis of different types of educational objectives in the famous T*axonomy* of Benjamin Bloom and his colleagues, and also by R. Gagne's analysis of different types of learning in T*he Conditions of Learning*, both of which imply a progression from simple to complex. See also the recent publications of the National Council for Vocational Qualifications in the United Kingdom, which operationalise this concept in terms of four levels.
19. For the original distinctions between formal, non-formal and informal education, see COOMBS, P.H. *et al.* (1973) *New Paths to Learning,* International Council for Educational Development, New York.
20. SQUIRES, G. (1987) *The Curriculum Beyond School*, Hodder and Stoughton, London, p. 48. The headings used in each of the three dimensions are derived from three United Kingdom writers on the subject, and therefore reflect that particular national context; they are given here only by way of example. Other systems might yield different headings, particularly in the *knowledge* dimension.
21. ARGYRIS, C. (1982) *Reasoning, Learning and Action,* Jossey-Bass, San Francisco; SCHON, D. (1987) *Educating the Reflective Practitioner*, Jossey-Bass, San Francisco. Some of the recent psychological research on the nature of expert knowledge in professional fields such as medicine, law and engineering also points to a more complex concept of "practice" which does not simply derive from the application of "theory".
22. SNOW, C.P. (1964) *Two Cultures: and a Second Look*, Cambridge University Press, Cambridge.
23. SIMON, H. (1969) *The Sciences of the Artificial*, MIT Press, Cambridge, Mass.
24. CROSS, K.P. (1976) *Accent on Learning*, Jossey-Bass, San Francisco.
25. TOUGH, A. (1971) *The Adult's Learning Projects*, Ontario Institute for Studies in Education, Toronto; (1982) *Intentional Changes*, Follett, Chicago.
26. OECD (1983) *Policies for Higher Education in the 1980s, op. cit.*, pp. 164-187.
27. SQUIRES, G. (1986) *Modularisation,* Consortium for Advanced Continuing Education and Training of the Universities of Manchester and Salford, UMIST and Manchester Polytechnic, Manchester.

ANNEX

LIST OF COUNTRY STUDIES

The eleven case studies were prepared by the authors listed below, in accordance with guidelines prepared by the Secretariat and agreed with them. The case studies are available separately from the main report.

* * denotes study prepared within the relevant ministry;
* \+ denotes study prepared outside the relevant ministry.
  FR = French
  EN = English

+ CANADA (QUEBEC) (FR)
  M. Paul Inchauspé, Directeur-Général du Collège Ahuntsic, Montréal.

+ GERMANY (EN)
  Prof. Dr. Wolfgang Mitter, Director, Deutsches Institut für Internationale Pädagogische Forschung, Frankfurt-am-Main.

+ ITALY/ITALIE (FR)
  M. Pier Luigi Bongiovanni and M. Giorgio Allulli, Centro Studi Investimenti Sociali (CENSIS), Roma.

+ JAPAN (EN)
  Mr. Hideo Iwaki, Senior Researcher, National Institute for Educational Research, Tokyo.

* NETHERLANDS (EN)
  Mr. F.J.M. de Rijecke, Deputy Director, Policy Development for Secondary Education, Ministry of Education and Science, The Hague.

+ SWEDEN (EN)
  Mr. Mats Myrberg, National Board of Education, Stockholm.

+ SWITZERLAND/SUISSE (FR)
  M. Emile Blanc, Ancien délégué de la Conférence Suisse des Directeurs Cantonaux de l'instruction publique aux relations internationales, Berne/Genève.

+ UNITED KINGDOM (ENGLAND AND WALES) (EN)
  Mr. Jack Mansell, formerly Chief Officer, Further Education Unit (FEU), London, and Mr. John Millar, Consultants at Work, Ware.

+ UNITED KINGDOM (SCOTLAND) (EN)
  Mr. David Raffe and Dr. Nils Tomes, Centre for Educational Sociology, University of Edinburgh.

* UNITED STATES (EN)
  Mrs. Nevzer Stacey and others, Higher Education and Adult Learning Division, Office of Educational Research and Improvement, United States Department of Education, Washington, D.C.

+ YUGOSLAVIA (EN)
  Professor Vladimir Mužić, Faculty of Philosophy, University of Zagreb, Zagreb.

Responses to the activity were also received from the French Ministry of Education (M. J. Geoffroy) and from the Greek Ministry of Education (Mr. F.K. Voros).

WHERE TO OBTAIN OECD PUBLICATIONS
OÙ OBTENIR LES PUBLICATIONS DE L'OCDE

ARGENTINA - ARGENTINE
Carlos Hirsch S.R.L.,
Florida 165, 4º Piso,
(Galeria Guemes) 1333 Buenos Aires
Tel. 33.1787.2391 y 30.7122

AUSTRALIA - AUSTRALIE
D.A. Book (Aust.) Pty. Ltd.
11-13 Station Street (P.O. Box 163)
Mitcham, Vic. 3132 Tel. (03) 873 4411

AUSTRIA - AUTRICHE
OECD Publications and Information Centre,
4 Simrockstrasse,
5300 Bonn (Germany) Tel. (0228) 21.60.45
Gerold & Co., Graben 31, Wien 1 Tel. 52.22.35

BELGIUM - BELGIQUE
Jean de Lannoy,
Avenue du Roi 202
B-1060 Bruxelles Tel. (02) 538.51.69

CANADA
Renouf Publishing Company Ltd
1294 Algoma Road, Ottawa, Ont. K1B 3W8
Tel: (613) 741-4333
Stores:
61 rue Sparks St., Ottawa, Ont. K1P 5R1
Tel: (613) 238-8985
211 rue Yonge St., Toronto, Ont. M5B 1M4
Tel: (416) 363-3171
Federal Publications Inc.,
301-303 King St. W.,
Toronto, Ont. M5V 1J5 Tel. (416)581-1552
Les Éditions la Liberté inc.,
3020 Chemin Sainte-Foy,
Sainte-Foy, P.Q. G1X 3V6, Tel. (418)658-3763

DENMARK - DANEMARK
Munksgaard Export and Subscription Service
35, Nørre Søgade, DK-1370 København K
Tel. +45.1.12.85.70

FINLAND - FINLANDE
Akateeminen Kirjakauppa,
Keskuskatu 1, 00100 Helsinki 10 Tel. 0.12141

FRANCE
OCDE/OECD
Mail Orders/Commandes par correspondance :
2, rue André-Pascal,
75775 Paris Cedex 16 Tel. (1) 45.24.82.00
Bookshop/Librairie : 33, rue Octave-Feuillet
75016 Paris
Tel. (1) 45.24.81.67 or/ou (1) 45.24.81.81
Librairie de l'Université,
12a, rue Nazareth,
13602 Aix-en-Provence Tel. 42.26.18.08

GERMANY - ALLEMAGNE
OECD Publications and Information Centre,
4 Simrockstrasse,
5300 Bonn Tel. (0228) 21.60.45

GREECE - GRÈCE
Librairie Kauffmann,
28, rue du Stade, 105 64 Athens Tel. 322.21.60

HONG KONG
Government Information Services,
Publications (Sales) Office,
Information Services Department
No. 1, Battery Path, Central

ICELAND - ISLANDE
Snæbjörn Jónsson & Co., h.f.,
Hafnarstræti 4 & 9,
P.O.B. 1131 - Reykjavik
Tel. 13133/14281/11936

INDIA - INDE
Oxford Book and Stationery Co.,
Scindia House, New Delhi 110001
Tel. 331.5896/5308
17 Park St., Calcutta 700016 Tel. 240832

INDONESIA - INDONÉSIE
Pdii-Lipi, P.O. Box 3065/JKT.Jakarta
Tel. 583467

IRELAND - IRLANDE
TDC Publishers - Library Suppliers,
12 North Frederick Street, Dublin 1
Tel. 744835-749677

ITALY - ITALIE
Libreria Commissionaria Sansoni,
Via Benedetto Fortini 120/10,
Casella Post. 552
50125 Firenze Tel. 055/645415
Via Bartolini 29, 20155 Milano Tel. 365083
La diffusione delle pubblicazioni OCSE viene
assicurata dalle principali librerie ed anche da :
Editrice e Libreria Herder,
Piazza Montecitorio 120, 00186 Roma
Tel. 6794628
Libreria Hœpli,
Via Hœpli 5, 20121 Milano Tel. 865446
Libreria Scientifica
Dott. Lucio de Biasio "Aeiou"
Via Meravigli 16, 20123 Milano Tel. 807679

JAPAN - JAPON
OECD Publications and Information Centre,
Landic Akasaka Bldg., 2-3-4 Akasaka,
Minato-ku, Tokyo 107 Tel. 586.2016

KOREA - CORÉE
Kyobo Book Centre Co. Ltd.
P.O.Box: Kwang Hwa Moon 1658,
Seoul Tel. (REP) 730.78.91

LEBANON - LIBAN
Documenta Scientifica/Redico,
Edison Building, Bliss St.,
P.O.B. 5641, Beirut Tel. 354429-344425

**MALAYSIA/SINGAPORE -
MALAISIE/SINGAPOUR**
University of Malaya Co-operative Bookshop
Ltd.,
7 Lrg 51A/227A, Petaling Jaya
Malaysia Tel. 7565000/7565425
Information Publications Pte Ltd
Pei-Fu Industrial Building,
24 New Industrial Road No. 02-06
Singapore 1953 Tel. 2831786, 2831798

NETHERLANDS - PAYS-BAS
SDU Uitgeverij
Christoffel Plantijnstraat 2
Postbus 20014
2500 EA's-Gravenhage Tel. 070-789911
Voor bestellingen: Tel. 070-789880

NEW ZEALAND - NOUVELLE-ZÉLANDE
Government Printing Office Bookshops:
Auckland: Retail Bookshop, 25 Rutland Stseet,
Mail Orders, 85 Beach Road
Private Bag C.P.O.
Hamilton: Retail: Ward Street,
Mail Orders, P.O. Box 857
Wellington: Retail, Mulgrave Street, (Head
Office)
Cubacade World Trade Centre,
Mail Orders, Private Bag
Christchurch: Retail, 159 Hereford Street,
Mail Orders, Private Bag
Dunedin: Retail, Princes Street,
Mail Orders, P.O. Box 1104

NORWAY - NORVÈGE
Narvesen Info Center - NIC,
Bertrand Narvesens vei 2,
P.O.B. 6125 Etterstad, 0602 Oslo 6
Tel. (02) 67.83.10, (02) 68.40.20

PAKISTAN
Mirza Book Agency
65 Shahrah Quaid-E-Azam, Lahore 3 Tel. 66839

PHILIPPINES
I.J. Sagun Enterprises, Inc.
P.O. Box 4322 CPO Manila
Tel. 695-1946, 922-9495

PORTUGAL
Livraria Portugal, Rua do Carmo 70-74,
1117 Lisboa Codex Tel. 360582/3

**SINGAPORE/MALAYSIA -
SINGAPOUR/MALAISIE**
See "Malaysia/Singapor". Voir
« Malaisie/Singapour»

SPAIN - ESPAGNE
Mundi-Prensa Libros, S.A.,
Castelló 37, Apartado 1223, Madrid-28001
Tel. 431.33.99
Libreria Bosch, Ronda Universidad 11,
Barcelona 7 Tel. 317.53.08/317.53.58

SWEDEN - SUÈDE
AB CE Fritzes Kungl. Hovbokhandel,
Box 16356, S 103 27 STH,
Regeringsgatan 12,
DS Stockholm Tel. (08) 23.89.00
Subscription Agency/Abonnements:
Wennergren-Williams AB,
Box 30004, S104 25 Stockholm Tel. (08)54.12.00

SWITZERLAND - SUISSE
OECD Publications and Information Centre,
4 Simrockstrasse,
5300 Bonn (Germany) Tel. (0228) 21.60.45
Librairie Payot,
6 rue Grenus, 1211 Genève 11
Tel. (022) 31.89.50
Maditec S.A.
Ch. des Palettes 4
1020 - Renens/Lausanne Tel. (021) 635.08.65
United Nations Bookshop/Librairie des Nations-
Unies
Palais des Nations, 1211 - Geneva 10
Tel. 022-34-60-11 (ext. 48 72)

TAIWAN - FORMOSE
Good Faith Worldwide Int'l Co., Ltd.
9th floor, No. 118, Sec.2, Chung Hsiao E. Road
Taipei Tel. 391.7396/391.7397

THAILAND - THAILANDE
Suksit Siam Co., Ltd., 1715 Rama IV Rd.,
Samyam Bangkok 5 Tel. 2511630
INDEX Book Promotion & Service Ltd.
59/6 Soi Lang Suan, Ploenchit Road
Patjumawman, Bangkok 10500
Tel. 250-1919, 252-1066

TURKEY - TURQUIE
Kültur Yayinlari Is-Türk Ltd. Sti.
Atatürk Bulvari No: 191/Kat. 21
Kavaklidere/Ankara Tel. 25.07.60
Dolmabahce Cad. No: 29
Besiktas/Istanbul Tel. 160.71.88

UNITED KINGDOM - ROYAUME-UNI
H.M. Stationery Office,
Postal orders only: (01)873-8483
P.O.B. 276, London SW8 5DT
Telephone orders: (01) 873-9090, or
Personal callers:
49 High Holborn, London WC1V 6HB
Branches at: Belfast, Birmingham,
Bristol, Edinburgh, Manchester

UNITED STATES - ÉTATS-UNIS
OECD Publications and Information Centre,
2001 L Street, N.W., Suite 700,
Washington, D.C. 20036 - 4095
Tel. (202) 785.6323

VENEZUELA
Libreria del Este,
Avda F. Miranda 52, Aptdo. 60337,
Edificio Galipan, Caracas 106
Tel. 951.17.05/951.23.07/951.12.97

YUGOSLAVIA - YOUGOSLAVIE
Jugoslovenska Knjiga, Knez Mihajlova 2,
P.O.B. 36, Beograd Tel. 621.992

Orders and inquiries from countries where
Distributors have not yet been appointed should be
sent to:
OECD, Publications Service, 2, rue André-Pascal,
75775 PARIS CEDEX 16.

Les commandes provenant de pays où l'OCDE n'a
pas encore désigné de distributeur doivent être
adressées à :
OCDE, Service des Publications. 2, rue André-
Pascal, 75775 PARIS CEDEX 16.

72380-1-1989